Lindsay has a gift for putting feelings int[o] that can pierce our defenses and denials of our own feelings. openness about her struggles with feeling "not enough" helps us identify with her and with the biblical people she illuminates. Lindsay helps us confront the truth about our ongoing need for hope and grace, pointing us to Scripture and to Jesus' words and example for a path forward with God and within a trusted community. I needed to hear this again! Thank you, Lindsay!

—Diane Bahn, presenter, coach, PLI Learning Community coordinator

This book reads like a meaningful conversation with a best friend over coffee—a best friend who sees your struggles and identifies with the toiling of anxiety. Lindsay captures the exhaustion and vulnerability of anxiety while offering reassuring hope. *Take Heart* is relatable and accurate, with a loving, pointed reminder that our weakness is made strong in a God who seeks my unfaltering reliance on Him.

—Jessica Brashear, school counselor and director of the school counseling program at Concordia University, Nebraska

I am delighted that Lindsay has written about the ever-nagging emotion of anxiety. She comes beside the reader as a trusted and empathetic friend and mingles Scripture with her own story. Her book is a warm and inviting look into anxiety as it impacts our closest relationships. She leads the reader to ponder that anxiety has a redemptive and hopeful quality that God uses in other's lives. She spends the first section of her book laying out God's transforming love in the midst of our anxiety. The pauses between chapters for study and reflection are thoughtful and get at the heart of anxiety.

—Lisa Lessing, counselor and retreat leader

Many Christians wrestle daily with insecurity, perfectionism, and worry, and some experience seasons or a lifelong battle with anxiety and depression. *Take Heart* walks a beautiful balance of deep honesty about these struggles and the celebration of God's constant love, grace, and presence. Hausch doesn't dismiss the daily impact of anxiety and worry. Instead, she leans into how God can powerfully use it to direct us back to Christ and then into service to each other. This study doesn't give easy answers. Instead, it opens up important conversations and points us to God's Word and Sacrament for hope.

—Julianna Shults, program manager, LCMS Youth Ministry

In her book, *Take Heart: God's Comfort for Anxious Thoughts*, Lindsay Hausch reminds us that we are not alone. She tells of the importance of connection with both God and with the people that He has placed in our lives as a means of comfort and support. While painting a beautiful canvas of God's love for us, Lindsay gives us modern tools for coping with daily stressors: God, people, rest, and the courage to be vulnerable. For anyone who struggles with anxious thoughts, this is a must read!

—Nancy Barton, counselor, Lifeline Professional Counseling Services

Hausch imparts meaning, hope, and authenticity by sharing her journey while relying on grace during her most tangled moments with anxiety. Anxiety is not uncommon when we become overwhelmed by unexpected challenges we believe we have little control over. Reading *Take Heart* felt warm, peaceful, and gentle. Hausch shows how unnecessary it is to conceal our brokenness, because we do not need to be perfect or to refine our preparedness, because expectations will likely not match reality. Each chapter concludes with thoughts, verses for reflection, relevant questions, and a valuable, applicable activity for turning negative, weighted baggage into a toolbox for showing Christ's love to a world that is just as broken as we are.

—Marie Seltz, Candescent Counseling and Coaching

Anxiety is so often kept shushed as a private issue or disparaged as a lack of faith, and so it is wonderful that Lindsay Hausch has fought through her own life circumstances to bring the topic to the table for open, hope-filled conversation. For many believers, anxiety is a staccato spiral that forms the background soundtrack to their everyday attempts to "get it all together." Lindsay offers an understanding, sympathetic perspective and meets the noise of anxiety, beat for beat, with a steadying rhythm of grace and the resounding truth of who we are in Christ Jesus.

—Kristina Paul, deaconess, director of Care and Women's Ministries, Salem Lutheran Church and School

Packed with relatable, personal insight and a deep grasp of God's Word, this study fills you up without weighing you down. Lindsay speaks deeply and directly to anxious hearts. She meets participants in the realities of anxiety, equips you to reflect and to do the work of wrestling with your fears, and then invites you—at every turn—to rest in the finished and forever work of Jesus. This study is such a timely, compassionate, and truly helpful resource.

—Matt Popovits, pastor, author of *Tough Call: A Little Book on Making Big Decisions*

Take Heart

God's Comfort for Anxious Thoughts

LINDSAY HAUSCH

CONCORDIA PUBLISHING HOUSE • SAINT LOUIS

Published by Concordia Publishing House
3558 S. Jefferson Ave., St. Louis, MO 63118–3968
1-800-325-3040 • www.cph.org

Manufactured in the United States of America

1 2 3 4 5 6 7 8 9 10   30 29 28 27 26 25 24 23 22 21

THIS BOOK IS DEDICATED TO
Nathan, my blonder half.
God smiled when He wrote us together.
& Kathryn, soul sister extraordinaire.

CONTENTS

INTRODUCTION

Before I tell you what this book is about, I want to tell you what it isn't.

This book will not tell you that if you have more faith, you can overcome anxious thoughts or that your anxieties indicate lack of faith or spiritual immaturity. This book will not make you feel ashamed or alone in your struggle with anxiousness. That is because I personally struggle with anxious thoughts. Every. Single. Day.

Yes, friends, rather than the all-knowing expert, I'm the girl who is going to walk beside you and gently nudge you to consider that your anxious thoughts can be the very place where you can get to know God, and yourself, better.

When we stop asking if our faith is big enough, when we stop feeling the need to behave like we have it all figured out, when we are at the end of ourselves, we can encounter God. He is patiently waiting.

When I found out that I was going to write this book, I thought it was perfect timing. My two girls were old enough to be in school, so I would have time and space to relax and let my creativity flourish!

Like the best stories, my life took an unexpected detour.

A pregnancy test revealed "surprise!" Although our son, Bowden, took us by surprise, we know that he was always a part of God's plan. Of course, God's plans for us are often more challenging, but always better. Soon after we learned our family would be growing, my husband received a call to a different church, which he accepted, and our family relocated. We sold one home and bought another one in a few short months, then we settled into our new community. A few months later, we welcomed our son, Bowden, into the world, and then I was readmitted into the hospital for a week with preeclampsia. For two months following, I suffered from daily chronic migraines. When Bowden was six weeks old, he was hospitalized with RSV. In March, the girls' school went to remote learning, and I, like many parents throughout the world, took on a new role as homeschool teacher. And as I was writing the final chapter, my sister was diagnosed with breast cancer.

These personal struggles drove me again and again to the feet of Jesus. Many times, I decided I would quit writing. I was tired. It was too hard. Who was I to write a book, anyway? Some moments, I felt like an anxious mess.

But God would not let go of me, and He imparted to me His message of grace and comfort again and again.

I wanted to write a book about how God can use our struggles and anxious thoughts to draw us closer to Him and to equip us to provide hope and encouragement to others. What I didn't know was that before I could write this book, God had more for me to learn about this topic.

These words for you weren't written in my peaceful home

while the kids were at school. Rather, each word, paragraph, and chapter was wrestled over and fought for in the mess of life as I turned again and again to God's Word for strength and wisdom.

I think God is challenging each of us to be vulnerable in the places where we feel unqualified and in the moments when we're close to giving up. Rather than cleaning up or puffing up so we can appear like we have it all together, He wants us to be vulnerable about our insecurities, uncertainties, disappointments, and desperation. In our anxious hearts as we come to the end of ourselves, we can see that our weakness is the place for His grace.

> My grace is sufficient for you, for My power is made perfect in weakness.
>
> (2 Corinthians 12:9)

For many of us, anxious thoughts are an everyday reality. But what appears to be our defeat can be transformed into purpose as God is with us in our struggle, comforting us, using us to love and comfort others.

When our anxiety makes us feel stalked by fear, dizzy with doubt, and hemmed in by our own hurtful thoughts, God can draw us to Himself and lead us to safety, not once, but every time it happens. As we seek Him moment by moment, in the vortex of life's disappointments, distractions, and the anxieties that result, God perfects our faith through His grace. It is always enough.

PART I

THE HEART
OF
GOD
(UP)

Oct 6

CHAPTER 1

REPURPOSED BY GRACE

Sitting in the dark movie theater, my eyes were fixed on the screen, but my thoughts were somewhere else. My mind was spinning through the worst possible outcomes of an unknown future.

A pipe burst on Mother's Day. Early the next morning, the abatement team began packing everything, moving it into storage, and ripping up floors as they disassembled our house. Could water do that much damage? Like aftershocks of an earthquake, my life shifted and shook, turning normal on its head. That is how I came to be in this cold movie theater on a hot June day, stressed and focused on anything but the plot unfolding on the screen in front of me.

We'd been in a hotel for a month, and it was not working. Progress on our home was haltingly slow, and dragging my two-year-old, my five-year-old, and our family dachshund down five floors and through a lobby for regular potty breaks for the dog's tiny bladder was using my last reserves of patience.

My life felt out of my control—and feeling out of control makes my anxiety flare like fireworks on the Fourth of July.

Maybe you can relate.

A job loss, emergency house repairs, a car accident, a hospital stay, or an unexpected bill. If life were predictable and we were always in control of it, anxious thoughts would be nonexistent. But nothing about life this side of heaven is predictable or easy, so anxious thoughts persist.

The movie flashed before my eyes, and panic raged within. As my thoughts raced, my body responded with cold sweat and shallow breath. My leg bounced up and down, up and down, to the tempo of my chaotic thoughts. My shell of a body felt slow and stiff and desperate for air, even as it thrummed with the racing pulse of fear and dread.

It took a moment for me to realize that my husband, Nathan, had leaned over and positioned his face close to mine. I had forgotten he was beside me. Didn't know he was watching me. He put a heavy hand on my leg. He slowed the tremble, little by little, firmly steadying my buzzing body. "I love you," he whispered. "We'll get through this."

My breathing slowed, my leg went still, the roiling thoughts eased. I looked in my husband's cool blue eyes, and I was there, in that moment, with him. I was no longer completely alone and lost in a swirl of anxious thoughts about the future.

FACING OUR ANXIOUSNESS

As someone who has struggled with obsessive-compulsive disorder, social anxiety, and generalized anxiety since childhood, I did not write a book that tells you that overcoming anxious thoughts is as simple as having faith and praying "enough," nor do I assert that the presence of worry and anxiety is an indication of your lack of faith. Instead, what I seek through this book is to communicate that my anxiety is the very thing God uses to remind me of my need for Him.

I invite you to consider that your struggle can be a training ground for spiritual growth and endurance as you learn to release your grip on control and find peace in knowing that God is in control. But first, I want to address some of the misunderstandings that can arise when anxiety is the topic of discussion.

Too often, our society speaks of anxiety as though it's a knitted poncho with a "one-size-fits-all" label that can casually cover the shape and subtleties of each person's experience. (Whoever thought a sweater without armholes was a good idea anyway?) It's important to acknowledge from the get-go that if your anxious thoughts are compromising your quality of life, then I highly recommend seeking the support of a medical professional and exploring whether medication, therapy, or a combination of the two would be beneficial for you. This girl (pointing to myself here) has benefited from both, and I don't see any book as a replacement for that.

Whatever your experience, there is a reason you have picked up *this book*. You, dear reader, need to hear the whisper "we'll get through this" and be reminded that you aren't alone in your anxious thoughts.

You picked up this book because you understand what it's like to be lost in a swirl of accusing thoughts, stressed over undone tasks, or consumed by "what-ifs?" All of that causes you to miss the life story that's unfolding right in front of you. You understand that it is possible to become so disoriented in your own thinking that you overlook the good gifts God has given you. You and I, friend, need a caring person who can remind us to seek our Father's face and remind us that He loves us.

> For God alone, O my soul, wait in silence, for my hope is from Him. He only is my rock and my salvation, my fortress; I shall not be shaken.
>
> (Psalm 62:5–6)

When I am overcome by anxious thoughts, it's hard to think or do *anything* except remember that I am deeply loved. I am loved despite my insecurities and contradictions. I am loved in the chaos of my fear and weakness, pride and arrogance, and insufficiency. This knowledge is a step toward understanding that I am utterly helpless but that God meets me in my mess. This is G.R.A.C.E. (God's Riches at Christ's Expense). *Grace* is God's love, forgiveness, and favor, given to us because of who God is: our heavenly Father, who created us; our Savior, who earned forgiveness for us by His death on the cross and resurrection; and the Holy Spirit, who sustains our faith and defends us. God's grace is something I will never fully grasp, but it comes to me in a whisper that cuts through accusing thoughts, reaches out in a hand that slows the thrum of unease coursing through me.

> For you know the grace of our Lord Jesus Christ, that though He was rich, yet for your sake He became poor, so that you by His poverty might become rich.
>
> (2 Corinthians 8:9)

God's grace meets us just as we are. He emboldens us to look up, to see beyond ourselves, even as anxiety threatens to suffocate hope. In the tension between our anxiety and God's grace, we can learn a dance with God that makes our stumbling uncertainty look like purpose.

God not only loves me—stressed out, anxious, and fearful mess that I am—but He also wants to use me. He wants to use you too. Our baggage becomes a toolbox for showing love to a world that is just as broken as we are.

> For by grace you have been saved through faith. And this is not your own doing; it is the gift of God, not a result of works, so that no one may boast.
>
> (Ephesians 2:8–9)

Yes, my anxiety humbles me and strips me of pretense. From this bare place, I am better equipped to share about God as I rest in who He is and not in who I am. Have you also experienced an opportunity to love the world in your most vulnerable moments? God provides us with the radical opportunity to use our hurt to help, and in the process, we experience more healing.

It should be straightforward. God sent His Son, Jesus, who humbled Himself for our sake. He experienced the same humanity we do. He had such great compassion for us that He went to the cross. He was mocked, abandoned, and abused. And on that cross, He died. He was the sacrifice so that we could be God's children. In the face of that kind of love, we should not hesitate to humble ourselves for Jesus in order to bear witness to others about God's love. But you and I know that the story doesn't end there. Because we are weak and flawed by our fallen sinful nature, it can get a little complicated.

Sin comes between God and us, and it clouds our perspective. It makes us turn inward so we want to rely on ourselves rather than looking through the cloud to God to help us out of our anxiousness. Sure, I want God to use me for His good, but I want Him to follow my script, which means I want God to fix all my problems, and I want to be loved and respected by others in the process. I'll take His grace and faith, but may I please have them on the side and let *my* agenda be the main course?

God's grace, a continuous and limitless gift received by faith, calls us to release our grip on control and trust Him to guide us. But because my sinful nature is involved, I am tempted to wrestle back control. At times, instead of resting in God's gracious gift, I fall back into the trap of trying to earn God's favor like gold stars. Can you relate?

QUEEN P AND WANNABE

In a world where worth is measured by accomplishments and image is improved with every little (or big) thing we get done, the *P*s can get in our heads like mythical sirens calling us into their trap. It's easy to live a life that is more about our activity than about God's grace for us. Too easily I fall into the trap of tying my worth to the things I check off my unending to-do list. As we read above, Paul writes in Ephesians that it's "not [my] own doing," but I can move around like it is.

I call this alter ego Queen P. Queen P is smugly satisfied

with herself as she plans, proves, postures, performs, and per-fects. As she pretends, protects, pleases, and pushes her way through life.

While most of these *P*s are impossible to avoid entirely, the real problem is when we use them to direct our decisions and focus away from God. When we become so consumed with our own ability to achieve perfection or appear perfect, we can fall into the trap of thinking that peace and happiness come from our achievements.

Which of the *P*s resonate with you? Do you plan, prove, posture, perform, perfect, pretend, protect, please, or push?

When these *P*s bully their way into our thoughts, what would happen if we could drive them out and arrive instead at a place of peace, of just being present in God's grace for us? When we embrace God's rhythm of reliability, we can see the disconnect between our need to control and our craving for what we need the most. When we are living loved by God instead of trying to earn approval, our lives are defined by purpose rather than pressure.

How does this gift of His love inform your everyday exis-tence? The next time the *P*s threaten to hijack your thoughts, what would happen if you hit *Pause* instead? We can let the pressures of our lives build to a deafening volume as we be-come too frenzied and distracted to enjoy the life unfolding be-fore us—or we can pause. We do not keep the world spinning. That's God's job! He is not only big enough to keep the world spinning but He is also capable of exquisite detail to know ev-ery hair on your head and to love you.

Pause for a minute to ponder whether you trust this God with your very life.

When you recognize the work God has already done and is doing this very minute, you can seize the opportunities for God to use you as you are.

The Japanese art form *kintsugi,* translated as "golden joinery," is the practice of mending broken pottery with a golden lacquer so the cracks are not hidden, but rather are highlighted and celebrated. (If you Google the word, you will see beautiful examples of this pottery.) When I think of shelves of *kintsugi* pottery, I imagine this is the way God sees each of us. The broken places are where He tenderly draws us close and makes us whole again. They are the places He empowers us to shine His glory. As with the pottery, our broken places are part of our history and not something we try to hide.

THE PULL OF THE *P*S

God's love pulls us out of the pressure cooker and into an open space where we can be ourselves:

> He brought me out into a broad place; He rescued me, because He delighted in me.
>
> (Psalm 18:19)

God's love rescues us and redeems us, making us His one-of-a-kind creations—cracked open, made whole again, complicated, but lovely—broken but beautiful. God's love empowers us to define beauty differently, helping us see broken things as the perfect material God uses to make us whole, repurposed by His grace.

It is love for others, for ourselves, for God, for life, that pulls us out of the need to do and draws us toward the gracious place where we can just *be*.

Be ourselves.

Be still.

Be with the person right in front of us—ourself, our loved one, our Lord as He comes to us in the Word—as Jesus invites us to come to His Table. We come broken, and He breaks Himself for us.

FACING GOLIATH

This may sound lovely, but how does this change our mental habit of pushing, proving, planning, and perfecting right now?

Maybe it doesn't.

Hold on—I'm going somewhere with this.

The Bible never promises that we will overcome our unhelpful thoughts. Nope, anxiety is not the Goliath we get to fell with one blow and shove out of our lives.

Too many books, blogs, and memes suggest this is possible, making us feel like fakes and failures. So we fall back into the trap of the *Ps, pretending* we have our negative thoughts under control. Everyone else has it figured out, right?

Wrong.

Overcoming anxiety is a constant tug-of-war between our flesh and our spirit. It is a tension that leaves our head spinning and our stomach in knots. But acknowledging that battle allows us to grab hold of the weapons God gives us to knock down the grizzly giants of anxiety that distract us and incite fear. Like David's five smooth stones, we grab hold of God's promises that remind us that we don't need to puff up to beat those giants; rather, we can rest in our smallness and rely on God's greatness.

Daily we can exercise our ability to stop anxiety in its tracks before we let ourselves get carried away by it. Paul's challenge to the Corinthians is a guidepost for this practice:

> We destroy arguments and every lofty opinion raised against the knowledge of God, and take every thought captive to obey Christ.
>
> (2 Corinthians 10:5)

We read about this in 1 Samuel 17. Saul offers David his own armor and sword. David puts it on but then steps out of it (1 Samuel 17:38–40). No, it isn't right. It weighs him down. It is clunky and ill-fitting. David might have looked more prepared wearing the royal armor. He could have pretended, for a minute, and borrowed some of the king's confidence. But conquering the giant meant embracing who he was called to be and trusting that God would work through it.

In this sinful world, anxiety is something we continually battle. You can defeat anxious thoughts for a while or pretend there is no longer a struggle. But not for long. Anxious thoughts campaign to replace the moment of quiet, reminding you that you can't pretend you've conquered it. When we leave our hearts unguarded, we make ourselves vulnerable again to the insecurities and uncertainties that threaten to invade.

When I was younger, I believed the accusations of my anxious thoughts. I let fear, doubt, and even paranoia bully me into the quietest corner of my soul. I let my anxiety trick me into believing that I wasn't good enough, that a counterfeit version of me was better. I pretended to be the girl a boy wanted to date, the daughter I thought my parents wanted me to be, the friend who said yes—even when those behaviors meant relinquishing my authenticity.

Anxiety tricked me into believing that I wasn't lovable and that I was all alone in my struggles. I planned, proved, postured, perfected. I pushed and pleased and squeezed myself into the different sets of armor that I thought would ultimately protect me. I pretended because I believed the lie that something was wrong with me.

Today, I have courage to see that God uses me just as I am to accomplish His purposes. It has been a journey of drawing near to Him as He draws near to me in His Word and sacraments of Baptism and His Holy Meal. He fills me with His Holy Spirit and places people in my life to point me back to His grace.

FACING ANXIETY AGAIN AND AGAIN

This growing understanding doesn't mean the battle is over. Throughout this book, we will explore how God's love can transform how we see ourselves through a rhythm of rest in relationship with God, in relationship with others, and as God equips us to share our gifts and experiences with the people He puts before us. I will share with you the ways I have learned to live well in spite of my anxiety and to trust that God's grace is sufficient. More than that, I have learned that God's power shines through my scattered heart to reflect a pattern of beauty into the world that speaks of His redeeming love.

God has equipped you to face your Goliaths—your fears and your struggles with anxious thoughts. This battle isn't one and done. We fight it day by day, sometimes minute by minute. And this ongoing battle is one way that God builds your faith and trust in Him. This battle for your mind is an opportunity to gain deeper insight into who He is creating you to be. I believe that over time, as you drag all your anxious thoughts into the light of God's love, you will grow more confident in your faith and more comfortable in your skin. Like a stone, smoothed and softened as it tumbles against the sand, God wears away the parts of us that don't belong and transforms us to be more like Him.

We can know the stillness and peace that come through relationship with God and calm the wave-beaten, scattered self that is pulled to and fro by life's circumstances. (See Ephesians 4:14.)

The anxious thoughts may always be there, but God doesn't let them pull us away. Rather, Jesus, "the founder and perfecter of our faith" (Hebrews 12:2), anchors us to Himself. In the storm of emotion, we can be still, squeeze our eyes shut, suck in our breath as we let the rough parts be worn away as our hearts become smooth, as God's grace draws close and whispers peace.

When we are able to see our weakness as the very place where God works in our hearts and lives, we can see that the battle is worth it for the strength and endurance it produces in our faith. We see how God reveals Himself most powerfully in our greatest place of vulnerability and weakness.

God wants to use us in our smallness, in our weakness, just as He did in the weakness of young David. God's greatness is on display when we acknowledge that we will never gain victory through our own strength or abilities. As we focus less on ourselves and more on God at work in our hearts, we can let go of the pressure to have everything figured out. We're all a work in progress. I am the person who in one moment listens to and prays for a friend in need, and in the next weeps and relies on the encouragement of another. And for some reason, God wants to use me exactly as I am.

He wants to use you too, exactly as you are.

The battle is ongoing, but know that the war is already won. God's love for us has the last word. So we shrug off the layers of pretension and protection and say, "I cannot go with these" (1 Samuel 17:39). Free of the weight of expectation, we are able to live more fully as the people God designed us to be.

REPURPOSED BY GRACE

Let's take a moment to dig deeper into what we discussed in this chapter and what God is showing us in Scripture.

KEY THOUGHT: Our anxiousness is where God accomplishes His purpose in our lives, drawing us to Him and giving us a story of grace to share with others.

Verses for Reflection

For in Him all the fullness of God was pleased to dwell, and through Him to reconcile to Himself all things, whether on earth or in heaven, making peace by the blood of His cross. (Colossians 1:19–20)

But God, being rich in mercy, because of the great love with which He loved us, even when we were dead in our trespasses, made us alive together with Christ—by grace you have been saved—and raised us up with Him and seated us with Him in the heavenly places in Christ Jesus, so that in the coming ages He might show the immeasurable riches of His grace in kindness toward us in Christ Jesus. For by grace you have been saved through faith. And this is not your own doing; it is the gift of God. (Ephesians 2:4–8)

Open Your Bible

Read 1 Samuel 17:33–40.

Questions to Consider

1. "God's riches at Christ's expense." What does that mean?

   _____

   _____

   _____

   _____

   _____

2. Lindsay says feeling "out of control" stirs her anxious thoughts. What are the things that stir up anxious thoughts for you?

   _____

   _____

   _____

   _____

3. Can you relate when Lindsay talks about the mental tug-of-war between anxious thoughts and God's promises? What does that look like in your daily life?

   _____

   _____

   _____

   _____

   _____

4. In 1 Samuel 17:33–40, David explains to Saul how he is able to face this Philistine giant. How did God equip David through his role as a shepherd?

   _____

   _____

   _____

   _____

5. Consider and share if there are unexpected ways God has used experiences in your life to equip you to face giants.

_____

_____

_____

_____

_____

6. In 1 Samuel 17:33–40, David refuses the king's armor, opting instead to use his slingshot and five smooth stones. What does this story lead you to consider in your own life? In what ways are you like David in this account?

_____

_____

_____

_____

_____

Activity

Consider which Bible verses help you when your mind feels attacked by anxious thoughts. Write one of these Bible verses below and commit to memorizing and reciting it when you face your own Goliaths.

_____

_____

_____

_____

_____

CHAPTER 2

REST: RECEIVE THE GIFT

My friend and I committed to sitting awhile, sipping lattes from ceramic mugs that felt heavy and solid wrapped in our cold hands. As we sank into cushioned chairs that lined the quiet sidewalk of Old Town, I relaxed into a rare moment when I didn't look at my phone or my watch. Our conversation wasn't rushed or interrupted like the ones we're accustomed to as moms with young children. Words came slowly and thoughtfully. Between sips, we exchanged secrets and fears like sweet morsels contrasting the wet salt of stray tears. The bittersweet beauty of honesty and connection feels so right, like a surprising gift.

After sharing our stories and holding each other's hurts, she reached across, covered my hand, and said, "You have a deep faith in Jesus, but Satan uses your anxiety to make you busy and distracted."

A truth I knew, but it was so powerful to hear it spoken aloud. It was a confirmation and reminder I needed.

I believe I got the Martha gene. You know, the harried woman in the Bible who did all the bustling, hustling, serving, and hurrying when Jesus came to visit. Like Martha, I struggle to follow Mary's example to just sit and be—with Jesus—with anyone, really.

When my anxiety comes a-knockin', this Martha girl is a flurry of activity. Are you the same?

Do you prep and perfect, plan and research? Martha was fortunate that Google and Pinterest didn't exist back then.

Lately, I've been in a stressful situation with absolutely nothing I can do to prepare. Maybe you've been in the same place. You see the potential for loss, disaster, heartbreak, or a hard good-bye, and you realize that no researching, planning, analyzing, cleaning, or cooking, no checklist, spreadsheet, or "how-to" book can prepare you for the struggle ahead.

At a certain time, each of us comes face-to-face with helplessness. And knowing we are helpless is a surefire way to get our anxiety doing overtime in overthinking and worrying. So what's an anxiety-prone girl to do?

It might be worth another look at the story of Mary and Martha:

> Jesus entered a village. And a woman named Martha welcomed Him into her house. And she had a sister called Mary, who sat at the Lord's feet and listened to His teaching. But Martha was distracted with much serving. And she went up to Him and said, "Lord, do You not care that my sister has left me to serve alone? Tell her then to help me."
>
> (Luke 10:38–40)

Yes, this sounds familiar. Like a crack in a windshield, Martha's anxiety makes her thoughts web and spread into fragments of "what if?" What if I don't cook a suitable meal for Jesus? What if my bread burns? What if the wine runs out? What if Jesus sees how messy my house really is? What if I am not enough? Each question makes her more and more frenzied, more and more distracted from what's actually happening until it combusts into her cry: "Lord, do You not care?"

Look back at your last anxiety-provoking situation. Was it a health scare, job loss, misunderstanding with a friend, or worry over your children? If we look at the "many things" that we are upset about in our own life, how much of it is needed and how much is it our minds scurrying down rabbit holes of "what if?"

Do you trick yourself into believing you will be able to rest when your world is finally in its proper place? Martha was distracted by preparing for Jesus' visit. She was so distracted that she missed the most important thing while it was happening before her eyes. Oh, dear Martha! I am the same! Like you, I miss life's precious unfolding as I'm hurrying and worrying about what I think my life should look like.

I'm brought back to those words my friend spoke in kindness between bites of a shared scone, "You have a deep faith in Jesus, but Satan uses your anxiety to make you busy and distracted."

We have another option waiting for us when we look past the distractions and clutter. Our Guest is so patient as He waits for our attention and affection. After Martha's holy indignation, Jesus replies to her:

> You are anxious and troubled about many things, but one thing is necessary.
>
> (Luke 10:41–42)

The answer is right in front of us, like a child's eager hand popping up in Sunday School as he begs to answer a question that is obvious yet elusive. What is the only thing that is needed for Martha? for us?

Jesus.

Martha was missing the Lord's very presence in her living room as she busied herself with preparing for Him.

It makes me think of the preparations we make at Christmastime—as we decorate, shop, wrap, and bake to celebrate our King's earthly arrival. Jesus, our King, came into our world in the most human way—an infant King, greeted by shepherds, with a bed of hay in a feeding trough for a makeshift throne.

I love Christmas. I especially love the season of Advent, which marks the period of anticipation as we prepare for Christ's birth. But there is a line that is easily blurred. On the one hand is mindful preparation and holy anticipation; on the other is blinding busyness that propels us through an obstacle course of distraction. It's easy to edge over the line from doing our best to plan and prepare to thinking that our preparations are so important that we get bitter, overwhelmed, and—you guessed it—anxious, as if our "doing" is what makes Christmas come. As if our "doing" is the glue that keeps our lives together. As if the world rests on our capable shoulders.

When we are fatigued from pretending that we carry our world, we slump and cry and believe that everything is crashing down around us.

But wait. Somehow, despite us, the world keeps spinning, and our lives keep unfolding without our orchestration.

Under the pressure we put on ourselves, or let other people or work or circumstances heap onto us, we can miss the point of what all of this is about. Jesus comes to us so we can be in relationship with Him. We need to take a step back from trying to save the world to see that, *so that He can be our one thing.*

Of course, when the answer is Jesus, it can become irreverent to add to it, yet it may feel too simple. "Yes, the answer is Jesus. I know. I've heard this before." So how does belief in Jesus inform my everyday anxious heart?

When I am busy preparing, I start to think that the future rests on me. And sometimes, that thinking bears out. Sometimes, we have a plan, and it works the way it's supposed to work. But what about the times when we do everything we can and things don't go our way? In this place of anxiety-inducing pressure, I am tempted to echo Martha's self-pity and indignation. "God, don't You care that I'm working really hard down here to keep the world spinning? Don't You care that I've done all the things a 'good girl' is supposed to do?"

Mary is forever remembered as the one who chose the good thing, to sit at Jesus' feet. But because Mary has been painted in this scene as obedient, we can forget that she was also human. Even when Jesus wasn't in Mary's home, I can imagine that she might have faced other occasions when she was challenged to choose between the pressure to prepare and intentional quiet time with God.

Despite our anxiety, we *can* learn the discipline of redirecting our fractured minds for a moment of solitude with Jesus. You and I can learn the discipline of centering on Jesus, even as our hearts and homes, our workplace and daily commute distract us with stress and over-activity. The demands of our daily lives are aspects of our different callings. Even as an anxiety-prone woman, I know that if I were to give up all the things that provoke my anxiety, I would be giving up many of God's good gifts in my life. The very nature of God's gifts of my husband and children, my home, community, and calling to write require hard work and tending. The unavoidable reality of a life worth living is that it is challenging and unpredictable and demanding.

I don't know about you, but as great as a tropical vacation would be, what I really need is rest that brings its restorative power into the rhythm of my everyday, ordinary life. I need the sort of rest that tucks itself into my routine like a power snack in my purse that I can unwrap during a tense day or moment when anxiety is crowding out my peace.

Of course, finding this rhythm of rest involves peeling back several layers. We need to take a break from our work to enjoy God and the people He's placed in our lives. But the Christian Sabbath means more than just a time to cease our work. Sabbath is about faith and anticipation as we center our hearts in the trust that God works in all circumstances to accomplish His will. Sabbath means we join other believers to offer our confession, worship, and praise and—here is the most important part—receive God's gifts of forgiveness and renewal in the Gospel and in the Lord's Supper.

The Sabbath mindset follows us into the rest of the week. This means that before we even begin to work, we trust that whatever the outcome, God will accomplish what He has planned to do, in our hearts and families, in our communities, in and through our churches, and in our world. Rest means releasing our own clutch on control as we trust that God is not just in control but also that He is wise and loving and works all things for the good of those who love Him. It means devoting time to reading and meditating on His Word, dedicating time to pray.

Sabbath rest prepares us to see the blessings instead of the burdens in our lives. It returns us into the world with purpose instead of a mindset that leads us to believe we can cobble together our lives through our own resourcefulness.

Every day, every moment, we choose to focus on Christ Jesus, or we choose to focus on the world's standards regarding how we should live, on social approval, public status, and cultural expectations. Focusing on Jesus means allowing Him to transform our lives. Sometimes, that means putting aside our goals, rejecting cultural expectations, and resisting pressure from others. Sometimes, it means the work we do looks different, looks countercultural. Always, our lives reflect efforts to obey Jesus' call to center our minds on Him in a world where worry, distractions, and to-dos can render us anxious, overwhelmed, and unsatisfied.

Transformed or Conformed?

Some research suggests that anxiety is a bad habit. The human brain is hardwired to detect thought patterns, and if our emotional responses to various situations are similar, then our brains learn to follow the same track. This means that past experiences and responses can actually shape future behavior. Researchers[1] found that in order to break out of these thought patterns, a person needs unstructured time to pursue creative thought. This can look like a long walk, quiet time to journal, or diving into an adult coloring book! Restful activities like these actually allow us to break out of our anxious response.

We tap into God's holy imagination as we put down the work of our hands to rest and enjoy His creation. To the apostle Paul, this discovery would not come as a surprise. He writes to the Romans:

> Do not be conformed to the pattern of this world, but
> be transformed by the renewal of your mind.

(Romans 12:2)

To be clear, Paul is not referring to rest that fits the world's standards of downtime and getaways, but rest that comes from God through the forgiveness Jesus gained for us on the cross. Sabbath rest is the result of worshiping God and receiving His gifts of forgiveness and reinforced faith.

Each of us is tasked with exploring healthy habits and activities that give our minds renewal and remove us from our anx-

---

1   Srini Pillay, MD, "Can you rewire your brain to get out of a rut? (Yes you can . . .)," *Harvard Health Publishing, Harvard Health Blog,* March 14, 2018, https://www.health.harvard.edu/blog/rewire-brain-get-out-of-rut-2018030913253/.

iety ruts. This means a life marked by prayer and time in God's Word. It means joining with other believers to worship, pray, and receive Communion, serving those in need as we share with them about God's love, and encouraging and challenging each other to show God's love to a broken world. Paul and other New Testament writers point to these as practices that form the Christian life.

But if we do these things to achieve the transformation Paul is talking about here, we can quickly edge into something like Martha's accusation, "Lord, don't You care that I am left to do all this work by myself?"

We can carefully observe all the practices that mark the Christian life and still fall into the trap of self-righteousness. The Pharisees turned God's desires for His chosen people into a giant to-do list and a rigid job description. Rather than enjoying a relationship with God, as Moses, Abraham, Joseph, Jacob, and David did, the Pharisees traded intimacy for morality. Morality that says we need to appear good, to do the right things to gain God's love, rather than enjoying and worshiping and receiving Him.

Even rest can become a religion. The world around us has wrapped rest in different packages, but all of them can teeter between authenticity and conformity. Mindfulness, meditation, and quiet time can lose their godly purpose in a world that takes truth and twists it to a deceiving degree. The secular world encourages rest that centers on self.

Some of the Pharisees confused the difference between God's invitation to rest and rest that conforms to man's standards. They created thirty-nine categories of the activities that were restricted, with subcategories that policed minute tasks, such as the number of steps they could take or how many letters they could write on the Sabbath.

But Jesus calls out the Pharisees on their false conformity when they try to apply their distorted practices of Sabbath onto His disciples. When the Pharisees jeer at Jesus' disciples for picking heads of grain as they were walking through a field, Jesus makes the transformational purpose of the Sabbath clear: "The Sabbath was made for man, not man for the Sabbath" (Mark 2:27). But Jesus also points out that the Sabbath is more than a holy day reserved for man's rest; He Himself is our ultimate rest: "So the Son of Man is lord even of the Sabbath" (Mark 2:28).

Sabbath keeping and rest are different for each of us, but ceasing our routine work is an integral part of our identity as God's children. This doesn't mean our anxious minds will always be coaxed to rest. It doesn't mean anxious thoughts won't distract us from the beauty unfolding right in front of us. But it does mean that we do our best to embrace and enjoy the imperfect rest that punctuates our busy lives. Sometimes, it's a week, a day of the week, or a morning we set aside. Sometimes, it's those snack-size moments we sneak into the daily grind.

The to-do lists, chores, people, and stress stick in our minds and divide it with a web of worry, but we find the "one thing" that's needed again and again as we recenter ourselves on Jesus. "One thing" is a prayer whispered in a bathroom stall or a Bible verse read on a cell phone in line at the bank. "One thing" is a deep breath and gentle word when we want to spit back a divisive retort. "One thing" is that small decision again and again to respond to Jesus and remember His grace.

Ultimately, our rest is imperfect and incomplete. That is why we need the Lord of the Sabbath. When Paul tells the Romans to "be transformed" (see Romans 12:2), he wasn't talking about a kind of transformation we can achieve for ourselves like the montage makeovers we see in rom-coms, where an awkward girl gets a new wardrobe, hairstyle, and makeup, and then, "Ta-da!" her identity is turned around Cinderella-style. To be sure, we are all fixer-uppers in need of total overhauls. But the transformation Paul refers to cannot be achieved with human effort.

Paul challenges us to "be transformed," or *metamorphoo*. There are only four times in the Gospels that we see the Greek verb *metamorphoo*, meaning "to change into another form." This is the same verb Matthew uses in the account of Jesus' transfiguration on a mountaintop. He describes how Elijah and Moses appeared with Jesus, and how Jesus' "face shone like the sun, and His clothes became white as light" (Matthew 17:2). We see a relationship between the transformation that Paul describes for us and the divine transformative power revealed in Jesus.

Too easily I'm tempted to look for a formula in my Bible for how to navigate my anxiety. "Do *X*, and you'll get *Y*." Oh, wouldn't that be nice! But what Jesus teaches me again and again is that this isn't an input-output kind of thing. I receive peace and renewal when I come to Jesus desperately thirsty,

41

trusting that He has the living water I need. When I am bone-tired from this wearying world, I've learned that the world's rest feels good, but it's a quick fix rather than life sustenance. Ultimately, I find true rest when I come to Him with nothing to offer but my broken self and nothing to do but trust. I come to Him with my fractured mind, and even for just a minute at a time, He makes it whole.

Rest is woven into the fabric of our identity because God planned it that way. Jesus did His ultimate work for our salvation. Our very identity rests in knowing we will never do enough or be enough. But because of God's Son, we are enough. We are transformed in the waters of our Baptism and the power of God's Word spoken over us. "We were buried therefore with Him by baptism into death, in order that, just as Christ was raised from the dead by the glory of the Father, we too might walk in the newness of life" (Romans 6:4).

Jesus finished His work and returned to His Father, and His still, small voice lives in us.

Yes, Immanuel, God with us, did the work for us on the cross. He sent the Holy Spirit to give us faith and sustain it. He comes to us in the sacraments—Baptism and the Lord's Supper—giving us forgiveness, full restoration, and full transformation. Now, we have God in us and a relationship with Abba, our Father.

In Jesus, we experience unity. We shout Jesus' battle cry from the cross, "It is finished" (John 19:30), again and again as the world tries to taunt us and tell us to prove our worth. Yes, we find Jesus, our one thing, in repentance and rest. We are made strong in quiet trust (Isaiah 30:15).

REST: RECEIVE THE GIFT

KEY THOUGHT: Jesus invites us to set aside our work and turn our anxious mind to Him for rest and renewal.

Verses for Reflection

For thus said the Lord God, the Holy One of Israel, "In returning and rest you shall be saved; in quietness and in trust shall be your strength." (Isaiah 30:15)

I appeal to you therefore, brothers, by the mercies of God, to present your bodies as a living sacrifice, holy and acceptable to God, which is your spiritual worship. Do not be conformed to this world, but be transformed by the renewal of your mind, that by testing you may discern what is the will of God, what is good and acceptable and perfect. (Romans 12:1–2)

Open Your Bible

Read Luke 10:38–42.

Questions to Consider

1. Isaiah 30:15 says, "In returning and rest you shall be saved." What does "returning" mean here? This is the verse in the English Standard Version (ESV). Use an online search engine or other Bible versions you have to read this verse in different translations. Do you see other layers of meaning?

   _____

   _____

   _____

   _____

   _____

2. In Luke 10:38–42, we see Martha frustrated with Mary for neglecting her responsibilities. Can you relate to Martha's frustration with Mary for not helping?

   _____

   _____

   _____

   _____

   _____

3. Jesus says to Martha, "One thing is necessary." What is that "one thing"?

   _____

   _____

   _____

   _____

   _____

4. How does Jesus' response reshape your perspective?

_____

_____

_____

_____

_____

5. How do you tend to turn Sabbath rest into a command rather than an invitation? How is God inviting you to think of rest differently?

_____

_____

_____

_____

_____

6. Reflecting on Romans 12:2, how can you renew your mind this week?

_____

_____

_____

_____

_____

Activity

What is one thing you could do to incorporate rest into the rhythm of your everyday life? Write it below. Remember to keep it small and measurable. Ask a friend to check in to see how you did.

_____

_____

_____

_____

_____

_____

CHAPTER 3

REST: A HOLY BALANCING ACT

We woke up a bit earlier than on most Saturday mornings, coaxing our girls out of their pajamas and into regular clothes. Nathan and I wanted to go to the farmers market as a family before I was off to a women's luncheon at a nearby church. Whenever we go to the market, we indulge in a pound of sweet peas and a flat of bright red strawberries, but it's the sense of community and festivity that keeps us coming back. We spent an hour together as a family that morning, sipping coffee, snacking on strawberries, and tapping our feet to live bluegrass music. Nathan and I laughed at our daughters' uninhibited dancing that inspired other children to get swept up in their own choreography, their bright smiles collected like helium balloons that bounced and bobbed in a spontaneous party. I silently bonded with other parents as we exchanged conspiratorial smiles and exaggerated gasps of joy.

As I explore the topic of rest, I've been taking time to observe it in my own life. Often, it feels hard to describe, but lately, when I am enjoying a restful moment, I pin it in my mind, like the ticket stubs and photographs I tacked to my corkboard when I was in high school. This memory of the farmers market was one such moment that I marked "This! This is rest."

We cut the morning short, herding the kids to the car so Nathan could drop me off in time for the luncheon. I kissed the family good-bye and looked forward to the few hours free of obligations to relax with other women and maybe learn more about myself. This was the kind of rest I had planned for and looked forward to.

The conference room was already crowded, but I found an empty chair at a table of unfamiliar faces. We exchanged polite conversation as I positioned my mouth into a smile and nodded robotically between uncomfortably long pauses. Finally, the speaker was introduced, saving me from my underdeveloped small talk skills. I pulled out my notebook, pen poised, as the woman with a trained bob and black pantyhose took the stage to polite applause. But as she began her talk about living a life of service, I felt increasingly unsatisfied and restless. It was as if I'd been transported back to high school math class. I tried to focus on the lesson, but I wasn't sure how to apply it to my life. Nonetheless, I sat straighter in the chair, resisting the temptation to sneak outside to sit under a tree and read a book on my phone. I had set aside precious time for this event. But rather than getting the rest and validation I longed for, I felt depleted and guilty for not getting enough of it.

I realize now that my expectations were unrealistic—something that happens when I try to orchestrate rest.

Moments of genuine rest can take you by surprise, like a fit of uncontrollable laughter that bubbles up in conversation or like running into an old friend. But then, there are times of rest and celebration you anticipate, like a piece of birthday cake you cover with foil and save in the fridge. You wait for the slice of time when you can dig in and savor each bite. Sometimes, the experience is as good as anticipated, but sometimes, it doesn't satisfy as much as you hoped.

Here are two questions to ask when planned rest leaves you unsatisfied:

1. What circumstances and activities guide me to a place where I can find peace and enjoyment?

2. What do I need from others to help me feel safe to rest?

Real rest for me comes in slices of time when I am free from the *P*s. (Yes, those pesky *P*s we talked about in chapter 1.) The ones that shift the focus back to myself and tempt me to do instead of be. When I set aside time to rest, but circumstances pressure me to plan, prove, perform, pretend, posture, please, perfect, protect, or push, then I'm left feeling not enough, drained, and restless. As an introvert with a tendency toward social anxiety, I recognize (now) that a women's luncheon isn't a space where my soul finds rest.

I invite you to lean in and think about the activities that have left you feeling less than rested because of the pressure of the *P*s. Are these still important commitments, or are they things you do because of your need to please others or because they're tradition? How can you give yourself the grace that God freely offers?

God's rest invites us to find the activities and relationships that bring us joy as we rest in the work He has already done. It invites us to step into His peace and presence to savor the life He has given us.

But a life punctuated by rest means more than just having intentional times of rest. It's also a way of moving through the world at a pace that is different from culture's tempo. As we accept God's invitation to rest, we can let it flavor who we are, what we do, and the things we say yes to.

This means giving our soul the same kind of tending and attention that we give to our physical health, our home, and our loved ones.

Perhaps it takes more.

Recently, I learned that a higher priority than my tasks of homekeeping, kid-keeping, husband-keeping, friend-keeping, and schedule-keeping is the need for soul-keeping.

In the Gospel of Matthew, we hear Jesus' perspective on the human soul. He tells His disciples that it's not only valuable but more valuable than the whole world: "For what will it profit a man if he gains the whole world and forfeits his soul? Or what shall a man give in return for his soul?" (16:26). In that light, I am challenged to reconsider the amount of time I dedicate to my spiritual needs.

SOUL-KEEPING

A keeper is someone who is tasked with looking after something or someone. Raise your hand; have you ever had a housekeeper do a deep clean of your house? Be still, my heart! There is no greater feeling! My problem is that there is no worse feeling than watching my kids undo that hard work in a hot ten minutes.

Yes, ma'am, a talented housekeeper has a way of finding the dust and grime that I overlooked. On the rare occasions that I have had such a person clean my house, I've learned that she truly has an eye for detail and an expertise that I do not.

I've seen the same laser focus in my niece, who plays goal-keeper on her soccer team. A ball shall not enter the goal area; the goalkeeper is charged with this one space to protect. A beekeeper pays close attention to his hives, making sure the colony is operating as it should. A bookkeeper has to be accurate and detail oriented.

In all of these, I see people who are tasked with one pur-pose. Driven by this purpose and intention, they successfully carry out their job.

I am sure we'd love to have this kind of focus and attention in all the aspects of our lives, but the reality is that many things clamor for our attention. But when we consider the value that Jesus places upon our souls, it seems that taking intentional soul time should make the top of our priority list. I believe that quiet time with God can be the perfect medicine to relieve our anxious thoughts.

While I'm sure this sounds great to all of us—in the midst of busy lives, how is it actually lived out?

Soul-keeping, for me, starts with waking early to read my Bible and to pray when the house is quiet. It's more sacred than the hot coffee in my mug and the splash of cream I pour into its black depths. My heart rests in the moments in the light of His Word for me.

Now, understand that this time has to start the day, before I get all my chores done, set up my coffee pot, and say no to other invitations so I can fall into bed a little earlier. I know that if I am not in bed by 9:30, my body will not cooperate with my five o'clock alarm, no matter how much I coax it. If you're not a morning person or you're in a busy season where this can't happen, then your quiet time will have a different shape. That's okay: our relationship with God isn't one-size-fits-all.

Time in God's Word is the spiritual bread that feeds and nourishes our faith and growth. In the Gospel of Matthew, Jesus wanders the wilderness for forty days without bread and water while being tempted by Satan. When Jesus resists Satan and refuses to turn stones into bread, He quotes Deuteronomy: "Man does not live by bread alone, but man lives by every word that comes from the mouth of the Lord" (8:3).

During Jesus' days in the wilderness, He resists physical hunger and Satan's temptation and responds to the devil's taunts with truths about God from the Scriptures. He resists Satan as He remembers who His Father is and what His promises are. This reminds me of the supernatural purpose of reading God's Word. Time in His Word nourishes us in the present moment, and it also helps our hearts to store up promises of God's goodness for future struggles.

For me, soul-keeping means saying no to commitments that fill me with dread and cause anxiety. Instead of gaining easy approval by saying yes to something I don't feel equipped to do well, I push through discomfort with a no. I want a life that is less cluttered with busy obligation in order to create space and clarity for the things God has prepared me to say yes to, things that would be pleasing to Him. Instead of falling into the trap of thinking that others can't get by without me, I remember that my time and talents are best spent doing the things God has planned for me to do, things that are consistent with my vocations and callings.

What this means in practice is that I don't accept every invitation to serve at my daughter's school, for example. But if someone asks me to meet with her to pray, I will rearrange my plans, arrange care for my kids, and go. Can you tell I'm speaking from experience? For me, there is no greater appointment than the chance to pray with a friend in need. You may read this and say, "Oh, that's not for me." Maybe that isn't what God is calling you to do. Maybe God intends you to be the always-ready school volunteer or the one who always is willing to be the hostess that opens her home.

When we say a "holy yes" to something the Lord has tasked us with, it doesn't mean that it will automatically be easy. God leads me to commitments that He equips and empowers me to do, all the while stretching me to grasp for more faith and trust in Him. Yes, soul-keeping is trusting that as we intentionally step into new commitments and challenges, God is stirring and stretching our hearts to meet the needs He calls us to fill. Have you heard the saying that God doesn't call the qualified—He qualifies the called?

We are all called to serve differently, to fulfill different vocations. Saying yes because you think yourself irreplaceable may mean taking up a spot someone else was called to fill. Saying yes because you think it's about your effort is not fulfilling a vocation God has given you.

Soul-keeping means that the things this world considers frivolous are essential to our growth and happiness. For me, that looks like less social media and more reading aloud to my kids. It looks like taking a break from the pressure of homework so I can hold my daughter and tell her she is already wholly loved. It means fewer after school-activities and more space for my children to talk and play, letting time and God form them as He sees fit.

As my husband reminds me, soul-keeping in an upside-down world means slow is fast and small is big: slow, meandering walks; small conversation over coffee or hot tea that grows cold; words from the Word that God plants in my heart slowly, morning after morning, like the raindrops that make a mustard tree grow.

Soul-keeping means remembering that God is the keeper of my soul. It means that even if I'm doing the right things, they cannot be done to earn favor, but simply as a response to Him. These things, these acts of service, done to give glory to God, are faith responses. Soul-keeping means knowing that nothing I do will make or break me, but that God is at work through me and in spite of me.

You have given me the shield of Your salvation, and Your right hand supported me, and Your gentleness made me great (Psalm 18:35).

LIFE IS GOOD BECAUSE GOD IS GOOD

There is a clothing brand that is famous for simple illustrations of happy stick figures enjoying life with three simple words that reinforce how good life is. The brand was created by brothers Bert and John Jacobs, who wanted to create art together. Their brand's name and vision were inspired by the challenge that their mom, Joan, gave them every night at the dinner table, "Tell me something good that happened today."

We are all uniquely different. I love asking people, "What excites you?" The answers are as different as the person I ask, but they have the same importance. What excites you? What is your good-life stick figure doing? For my husband, it's brewing beer. For my five-year-old, it's dancing. For me, it's gathering women around a table to visit and learn, to pray and talk about God's Word for us.

We make a mistake when we think that an action is not worth doing if it doesn't "accomplish" something, if it doesn't achieve a goal. We miss out if we underestimate the power of the intangible threads that hold life together, such as love, joy, and relationship—the ties that bind. We cheat ourselves when we believe that our time is always better spent checking things off of a task list or earning gold stars than it is finding joy in the present moment.

I tell my kids the adage I learned when I was young: "It's better to give than to receive." But as I grew up, I came to believe that this thinking is backward. It's better to receive than to give.

First, we must receive God's rest, His completeness, His perfect plan in order to give to a thirsty world. When we're giving to people who are thirsty for Jesus and we don't know Him, they will be unquenchable. We need to tap into God's spring of life, for the living water, for the rest and resources that equip us to live in an unquenchable world.

Another word for this is "abiding." Jesus illustrates this rest relationship to His disciples in the Upper Room at Passover just before He is arrested:

> I am the vine; you are the branches. Whoever abides
> in Me and I in him, he it is that bears much fruit, for
> apart from Me you can do nothing.
>
> (John 15:5)

Jesus knows He is leaving His disciples soon, and He knows that their remaining in relationship with Him is more important now than ever. In order for them to accomplish the great work ahead of them, they must have a relationship of continual dependence on Him.

With a five-month-old in the house, I've had to learn that rest begets rest. If I want a baby who sleeps well, then I have to be vigilant about his daytime naps and getting him down on time for bed. Our son is growing and learning every day, so he needs appropriate physical rest.

The Early Church experienced explosive growth after Jesus' resurrection and ascension, but before the apostles were sent out to do the work of His kingdom on earth, Jesus told them to return to the city and wait:

And behold, I am sending the promise of My Father upon you. But stay in the city until you are clothed with power from on high.

(Luke 24:49)

Abiding means waiting on God's timing, resting in His power, and trusting His provision. The disciples obeyed, and instead of launching into preaching and teaching, "they went up to the upper room, where they were staying. . . . All these with one accord were devoting themselves to prayer, together with the women and Mary the mother of Jesus, and his brothers" (Acts 1:13–14). Just as babies need rest in order to rest well, we see that Jesus' followers launch into their ministry first from a place of rest—as they receive and rest in God's strength.

ABIDING: A NEW KIND OF REST

A few days ago, a friend asked me for advice. She said, "Lindsay, I'm tired and drained all the time. I feel like I could burst into tears at any minute—and it's only Monday! I just had a whole weekend to rest and relax!"

I asked about her weekend and learned it had been full of good things: a church carnival, a big neighborhood barbecue, and an anniversary party for her in-laws. But then I pressed, "What did you do to rest?"

A long silence, and then she shook her head as big, tired tears rolled down her cheeks, "Nothing."

Sometimes, we just need to show up. We show up to family reunions, baby showers, work events, relatives' birthday par-

57

ties, and women's luncheons. Sometimes, we need to offer to make cupcakes, to host dinner, and serve our church and others. These things—like Martha's hosting—are part of the vocations God gives us.

The problem is that when we try to make these things the rest we need, we may feel unsatisfied, resentful, and unrested—ingredients for anxiety. When we look to our doing to define us, we lose touch with Jesus, who provides us with the true rest and peace our hearts need.

Abiding in Jesus is a way we remember who we really are. A tropical vacation or long nap has its place, but we receive true rest as we abide in who He is—our Savior, our Great Physician. We receive this rest as we rely on His promises and return to Him for the strength and wholeness found in the Word and the sustenance He offers in the Holy Meal. When we experience this soul-filling rest, we long for more. As Solomon put it, God has "put eternity into man's heart" (Ecclesiastes 3:11). God created us with a longing that only He can satisfy.

Isaiah promised a king who would govern us, provide for us, protect us. But instead of the far-off earthly king who is out of touch with his subjects, this King humbled Himself to dwell with us, gave up His life in order to give us the rest and peace we could not create on our own:

> For to us a child is born, to us a son is given; and the government shall be upon His shoulder; and His name shall be called Wonderful Counselor, Mighty God, Eternal Father, Prince of Peace.
>
> (Isaiah 9:6)

This King offers us counsel, strength, adoption, and peace. He gives us the ability to say no to the things that draw us away from Him and yes to the things that give us peace, restoration, and an affirmed identity in Him. Our King cares when we're anxious and stressed and wants to help us by calling us close so we may set our minds and hearts on Him.

In order to live as His children, we need time in His Word and prayer. We need time to rest and relish what He has done. We can eat strawberries from the stem, tap our feet to bluegrass music, get up and dance, and lose track of time. We can enjoy wandering thoughts by ourselves, conversations with friends, and adventures with our family. We can enjoy doing the things that God has created us to enjoy and know in our hearts that because we have a good God, this life is good too.

From this deep-seated identity as His called and redeemed children, we are able to participate in life with others with fresh eyes and full hearts to spill God's goodness onto people we come in contact with. As His children and heirs, we can let go of our anxious thoughts as we take time to enjoy the work God has done, and we have new vision to see the work He is doing in our midst.

REST: A HOLY BALANCING ACT

KEY THOUGHT: As we live a life that focuses less on the anxieties our culture tries to heap on us and more on the unchanging truth of God, we are able to live in a rhythm that is less anxious and more purpose filled.

Verses for Reflection

He has made everything beautiful in its time. Also, He has put eternity into man's heart, yet so that he cannot find out what God has done from the beginning to the end. (Ecclesiastes 3:11)

Come to Me, all who labor and are heavy laden, and I will give you rest. Take My yoke upon you, and learn from Me, for I am gentle and lowly in heart, and you will find rest for your souls. For My yoke is easy, and My burden is light. (Matthew 11:28–30)

Open Your Bible

Read Psalm 18:28–36.

Questions to Consider

1. What is the meaning of Ecclesiastes 3:11? How does it
    inform your thoughts about rest?

    _____
    _____
    _____
    _____
    _____

2. Matthew 11:28–30 talks about being yoked with God. What
    is a yoke? How can it provide rest?

    _____
    _____
    _____
    _____
    _____

3. In Psalm 18, David reminds us that God is our source of
    strength. How does acknowledging God's strength help
    us live more freely in the moment?

    _____
    _____
    _____
    _____

4. Have you experienced planned rest that left you dissatis-
   fied? What happened?

   _____

   _____

   _____

   _____

   _____

5. What are some things you feel God is inviting you to say
   no to? What is your holy yes?

   _____

   _____

   _____

   _____

   _____

6. How do you plan to abide in Jesus this week?

   _____

   _____

   _____

   _____

Activity

If you bake or cook, you're familiar with following recipes. What would your recipe for rest look like? Don't be afraid to be specific, and remember everyone's recipe will look different!

_____

_____

_____

_____

_____

_____

_____

_____

CHAPTER 4

ENOUGH TO SATISFY

It's so easy on a Monday morning to sing the chorus of "not enough." I wake up with the fuzzy feeling of not enough sleep. I go through my morning routine, chanting, "not enough time." I leave the house with not enough coffee, not enough patience for my kids, not enough gas to get where I'm going, not enough makeup for my not-enough face. It becomes an infection that contaminates my every thought and experience. As I sit in the stew of not enough, my mind reaches for more ingredients to feed the negativity and self-pity until I am fully steeped in ingratitude. It's the perfect recipe for a bad mood and a bad day.

The negative spiral of not enough isn't isolated to Monday mornings. When I begin to go down the rabbit hole of resentment in my relationships, I can sing the ballad of not enough about the people I love most, singing the blues about all the ways they don't meet my needs. And if I can feel that resentful of the people I love and live with, you can imagine how that negativity bleeds into my feelings toward strangers who leave shopping carts in my parking space and don't hit the gas when the light turns green.

Not enough is a shape anxiety takes in our lives. It burrows into our hearts and resurfaces unbidden, coming between us and God. It blinds us to God's activity in our lives and suffocates our trust beneath a malaise of doubt. Throughout the Old Testament, we see this anxiety bubble up in the Israelites. God performs astounding feats for them, freeing them from slavery in Egypt, miraculously dividing the Red Sea for their safe passage, going before them in a pillar of light to lead them through the wilderness. Yet the minute they feel discomfort, weariness, or uncertainty, the grumblings of not enough begin.

When they grow hungry in the desert, they grumble against Moses and Aaron, "We should have just stayed and died in Egypt, where we had pots of meat and bread" (see Exodus 16:3). In response, God rains down bread from heaven. All they have to do is pick it up and eat it. Then, not a chapter later, when they are short on water, the Israelites are at it again with their murmurs of not enough, questioning Moses, "Why did you bring us up out of Egypt only to die of thirst?" (see Exodus 17:3).

How quickly they forgot God's willingness and ability to provide! But my own ungrateful heart echoes their ungrateful cries, raising the same chorus of doubt and desperation when I get caught up in my own thoughts of not having what I think I need. Too easily I sink into the despair of the moment rather than standing on tiptoe to look back and remember all that God has done to bring me where I am.

Can you relate to this ballad of not enough? Is it a chorus that repeats on Monday mornings or a tune that's stuck in your head—the words resurfacing in inconvenient moments? Maybe you have good reasons to feel like life is not enough right now. Maybe you're walking through a difficult divorce, a debilitating diagnosis, or the death of a loved one. Maybe you're in a season of not enough as you stretch to meet the demands of your job, your husband, or your children, and there just isn't enough time, money, or energy to meet their needs and your own. Whatever your tune of not enough sounds like right now, let's pause to acknowledge it.

The ache of desperation and need is real. It beats like a death drum, drowning out and distracting us from God's goodness and the good in our life. The feelings are real, and the difficult experiences that lead you to this place are also real. The anxiety over not enough that keeps you up at night and hijacks your thoughts during the day is painful and valid.

Too often, I see and hear messages that try to put the Jesus bandage over wounds rather than spending time with people in their hurt. We see in the Bible that Jesus doesn't put a bandage on the hurting—He enters the lives of the suffering and sits with them and touches them and cries with them.

Sometimes, the very thing we need in our own place of not enough is someone with enough time and compassion just to sit with us and gently help us see things with fresh eyes. Sometimes, this looks like abiding with God in quiet as He lovingly removes the thorny thoughts that plague and push us into a scarcity mindset.

God provided for the thirsty Israelites when He instructed Moses to "strike the rock, and water shall come out of it, and the people will drink" (Exodus 17:6). After this, Jewish tradition says that the rock followed them as their water source. But God was up to more than just offering them a temporary fix for their human need. Paul explains to the Church in Corinth that the Israelites "drank from the spiritual Rock that followed them, and the Rock was Christ" (1 Corinthians 10:3). God provides "spiritual water" by means of the Rock that ultimately will be the cornerstone of the Church in the person of Jesus.

WATER THAT'S ENOUGH

In John's Gospel, we see Jesus' loving attention and gentle guidance as He sits with a Samaritan woman at Jacob's well. When I say "a Samaritan woman," I realize these words could pass by without the significance they had in that culture and time in history. First, it was not customary for a Hebrew man to talk to a woman in public. But more than that, as a Samaritan, this woman was considered socially off-limits. Samaritans were branded as mixed-breed foreigners whom Jews deemed unworthy to be near, let alone to sit and speak with.

In this story, Jesus Himself experiences "not enough" in own His circumstances. John explains that the Teacher and His disciples were on a long journey from Judea to Galilee. To get there, "He had to pass through Samaria" (John 4:4). Imagine a morning-long hike on rocky and dusty terrain, the sun beating on your back, no food or water, in a neighborhood that was considered the wrong side of the tracks. The disciples go to get food and leave Jesus sitting beside the well, wearied (John 4:6). Are you getting the picture? Jesus was hot, tired, hungry, and thirsty. For me, that is a recipe for a very bad mood, but not for Him. No, Jesus uses His own human need to connect with a person in need and to illustrate our spiritual thirst for something more than what this world can offer.

"Give Me a drink," Jesus requests (John 4:7). His simple appeal is rife with meaning, and the Samaritan woman feels its weight.

She responds, "How is it that You, a Jew, ask for a drink from me, a woman of Samaria?" (John 4:9). She skips pleasantries and bluntly asks Jesus, "Why *me?*" Me: an inferior woman. Me: a foreigner. But we can scratch even deeper. This Samaritan woman is drawing water in the heat of the day rather than early morning, when the other women of the community are there. She is avoiding social interaction and no doubt plenty of scrutiny.

Many biblical scholars drive home the point that this woman has had five husbands, and the man she currently lives with is not her husband. I wonder, though, if when we zoom in on these details, we distance ourselves from her. We don't know why she is living the way she is. But we do know that this woman is living a life of not enough. John reveals that she herself is "not enough"—yet here is Jesus coming to her.

Rather than dwelling on her question about her ("why me?"), Jesus makes it about Himself: "If you knew the gift of God, and who it is that is saying to you, 'Give Me a drink,' you would have asked Him, and He would have given you living water" (John 4:10). Jesus tells her about the living water that comes only through Him. As they continue to talk and Jesus reveals Himself as the Messiah that both Jews and Samaritans are waiting for, we see a total shift in this woman's perspective. She is still a woman, a Samaritan woman, still has a questionable past, but as Jesus helps her understand who He is, the circumstances of her not being enough are no longer unscalable walls.

Jesus does not remove the difficult circumstances of her life. But now her focus shifts from her own needs to the needs of her community. She abandons her water jar and returns to her village to tell others about her encounter. We witness a woman once isolated now reunited with her community. We see a woman once preoccupied by her own physical need for water now thinking only about witnessing to the living water that comes through Jesus. Her lack is still present, but her longing for Jesus, the Christ, is greater. Over the course of a conversation, she is transformed to see that her great spiritual thirst is fully satisfied in Jesus.

I could stop here, and it would still feel like a Jesus bandage. The Samaritan woman encounters Jesus, her life and perspective are transformed, and she lives happily ever after. That's how we should feel too. It's tidy and simple, isn't it? *Did it work?* If it were so simple, you wouldn't be reading this book.

The living water Jesus provide does not eradicate our earthly needs or cancel out the complicated circumstances of our lives. I believe the chant of not enough can persist in a chorus of anxious thoughts even when we're living the abundant Christian life, because we are created for a relationship of dependence on Jesus.

We don't get to see the rest of this woman's story or that of the Samaritans who put their faith in Jesus that day. I am certain it wasn't happily ever after, because their lives were still their lives on earth. As followers of Jesus, we still live in the tension between His enough and a world that cannot satisfy.

Friends, I know and love God. Some would think that as the pastor's wife, I would have my life as a follower of Jesus all sorted out. But I get thirsty, hungry, and crave burgers and lattes. I long for love and validation, an uninterrupted nap, and someday, a beach vacation. I scarf a pint of ice cream as I binge watch a favorite show and feel so full I could burst, and yet so, so empty. I know Jesus is the Messiah, but I turn to worldly comfort out of habit and a hidden hope that this time it might give me the fix I need.

Where does that leave us? Just as the Samaritan woman returns to her complicated life, we also wrestle with how to find satisfaction in the living water Jesus offers—as we refill our bottles again and again at the water cooler, as we walk through the world in socks that have holes, and as we live with pesky people who don't always emulate the peace of Christ. In our real world, living our ordinary lives, where things wear out and run out, how can we experience the living water that slakes our thirst once and for all?

First, a practical question we should address: What is this living water Jesus is talking about? I was never good at chemistry, but one lesson that stuck was that water comes in three forms: solid, gas, and liquid. But living water? A water that doesn't run out or run dry? Nope, my chemistry teacher never covered that one. To grasp what this living water is, we need to unpack more of Jesus' conversation with the Samaritan woman.

After Jesus reveals His knowledge of her difficult past, the woman shifts her focus from herself as she asks about the true place to worship God: "Our fathers [the Samaritans] worshiped on this mountain, but You say that in Jerusalem is the place where people ought to worship" (John 4:20). In response, Jesus tells her of a time when people can worship God any-where—everywhere: "But the hour is coming, and is now here, when the true worshipers will worship the Father in spirit and truth" (John 4:23). Here, Jesus hints about where this living water comes from—the Spirit of truth.

Later in the Gospel of John, Jesus speaks of living water in His proclamation on the last day of the Feast of Booths, "Who-ever believes in Me, as the Scripture has said, 'Out of his heart will flow rivers of living water'" (John 7:38). John goes on to explain that Jesus is talking about the Spirit, "whom those who believed in Him were to receive" (v. 39).

The Bible makes it clear that the promised spring of living water is the Holy Spirit, which the disciples receive at Pentecost after Jesus is crucified and resurrected and had then ascends to be with the Father. Just before Jesus goes back to the Fa-ther, He tells the disciples about the promised Holy Spirit, "I will ask the Father, and He will give you another Helper, to be with you forever, even the Spirit of truth, whom the world cannot receive, because it neither sees Him nor knows Him. You know Him, for He dwells with you and will be in you" (John 14:16–17).

Rather than in a temple or behind the curtain in the Most Holy Place, the Spirit of God will dwell in us, in our hearts. We receive the Spirit of God through Jesus: through His Word spo-ken to us (Acts 10:44–48) and in the waters of Baptism (Acts

2:38). This does not change our present reality, but it transforms the way we experience it. Yes, the reality is that cars break, the earth shakes, bodies slow, debt grows, war divides, loved ones die—yet God did not watch from a distance. Rather, He sent His Son to be with us so that His Spirit could be in us so that no matter the hurt, God is with us, refreshing us, reminding us that we are not alone. We get to experience life with Him as He renews our perspective and refreshes our thirsty souls. This means that the old chorus of not enough will still rumble in our hearts as we rumble with a broken world, but God's Spirit within us offers a spring of hope and renewal as we shift our thoughts and hearts back to Him.

God's Spirit in us through faith in Jesus is God's ultimate promise for anxious thoughts—but it doesn't come in the tidy, moralistic package for sale in a Christian gift shop. Instead, it comes in a real and gritty relationship with a Savior who gave His tears, sweat, blood, and ultimately, His life. His promised Spirit enters not just the tidy parts of our hearts but also the shadowy and shameful places, the places where loss and hurt have carved out dark and hollow shells. Jesus' living water comes like grace and makes dead things come alive again.

Ezekiel prophesies about this life-giving water that begins as a trickle from the altar and gushes into a river that brings life and renewal to everything it touches. God the Father gives us Jesus, our Rock, and from Him bursts forth the living water of the Holy Spirit, which gives us life.

> And wherever the river goes, every living creature
> that swarms will live, and there will be very many fish.

For this water goes there, that the waters of the sea may become fresh; so everything will live where the river goes.

(Ezekiel 47:9)

ENOUGH TO SATISFY

KEY THOUGHT: Anxious thoughts can take the shape of the phrase "not enough," as sickness, crime, conflict, and disaster threaten our security. But while our earthly experience will always come up short, we experience Jesus' promise of enough through the Holy Spirit, which fills the ache in our hearts with His peace.

Verses for Reflection

These things I have spoken to you while I am still with you. But the Helper, the Holy Spirit, whom the Father will send in My name, He will teach you all things and bring to your remembrance all that I have said to you. Peace I leave with you; My peace I give to you. Not as the world gives do I give to you. Let not your hearts be troubled, neither let them be afraid. (John 14:25–27)

But if Christ is in you, although the body is dead because of sin, the Spirit is life because of righteousness. If the Spirit of Him who raised Jesus from the dead dwells in you, He who raised Christ Jesus from the dead will also give life to your mortal bodies through His Spirit who dwells in you. (Romans 8:10–11)

Open Your Bible
Read John 4:1–42.

TAKE HEART

Questions to Consider

1. Where are you feeling that life is not enough?

   _____

   _____

   _____

   _____

   _____

2. How is the peace that Jesus offers in John 14 different from what the world offers?

   _____

   _____

   _____

   _____

   _____

3. In John 14, Jesus refers to the Holy Spirit as "the Helper." What words are used in other translations and throughout the Bible? Which do you most identify with and why?

   _____

   _____

   _____

   _____

   _____

4. How do you think Romans 8:11 relates to the living water Jesus promises the Samaritan woman in John 4?

   _____

   _____

   _____

   _____

   _____

5. In John 4, we see the Samaritan woman's perspective transformed by her encounter with Jesus. How does time with Jesus help you in the places of not enough?

   _____

   _____

   _____

   _____

   _____

6. What does your personal time with Jesus look like? How would you like it to look different?

   _____

   _____

   _____

   _____

   _____

Activity

Take a moment to reflect on the ways God is actively working for your good in your life right now. Write down one way that you see Him at work in difficult circumstances. Pray that God would give you "eyes to see" the ways He meets you in your present needs.

_____

_____

_____

_____

_____

_____

CHAPTER 5

ENOUGH TO GROW

Not only do we hand over the anxiety of "not enough" to God, turning to Him again and again, but somehow, we also see God use those very places of "not enough" to show us His abundance and to ultimately turn our suffering into purpose. Yes, in the places of our suffering, God provides enough to quench our thirst today and assures us that He will quench our thirst in the days to come, even through unimaginable circumstances.

Maybe you've heard that God can use your struggle for good (see Romans 8:28), but in the day-in, day-out grind when life's problems are bigger and more complicated than you can wrap your mind around, these words sound trite. The words "God can use this for good" can become a platitude that loses its meaning on the lips of well-intentioned people or people who say it to avoid getting too close to the pain and discomfort of another. "God can use this for good" is a terrible as a balm in vulnerable conversation, and it works more as a bandage to cover the unpleasantness and messiness of real life.

But let's explore what this cliché actually means. Understanding how God works in our wounds to accomplish His good purposes can propel us through difficult experiences where we feel the anxiety of doubt and not enough. In such times, we can look to Jesus to perfect our faith (see Hebrews 12:2) and rely on the Holy Spirit to supply us with enough faith to get through it.

Horatio Spafford is famous for penning the song "It Is Well with My Soul" (also known as "When Peace like a River"), but he wasn't an aspiring hymnwriter. Spafford was a prosperous lawyer and devout Christian who lived comfortably in Chicago with his wife and four daughters. In 1871, the Great Fire broke out, devastating the entire city and causing Spafford to lose much of his wealth. A couple of years later, his family planned a vacation in Europe. Business delayed Spafford, so he sent his wife, Anna, and their four little girls, Annie, Maggie, Bessie, and Tanetta, ahead of him on the ocean liner *SS Ville du Havre*. En route, the liner was hit by a British vessel and quickly sank. Anna was saved, but their four daughters drowned. Some days later, Spafford received a cable from her when she landed in Wales: "Saved alone. What shall I do?" Spafford quickly left Chicago to meet his wife. As he crossed the Atlantic, the ship's captain notified Spafford as they passed near the place where his daughters had drowned.[2] Over this spot, he wrote:

> When peace, like a river, attendeth my way;
> When sorrows, like sea billows, roll;
> Whatever my lot, Thou hast taught me to say,
> It is well, it is well with my soul.

---

2   American Colony, https://www.loc.gov/exhibits/americancolony/amcolony-family.html. Accessed September 8, 2019.

Though Satan should buffet, though trials should come,
Let this blest assurance control,
That Christ hath regarded my helpless estate
And hath shed His own blood for my soul.

He lives—oh, the bliss of this glorious thought;
My sin, not in part, but the whole,
Is nailed to His cross, and I bear it no more.
Praise the Lord, praise the Lord, O my soul!

And, Lord, haste the day when our faith shall be sight,
The clouds be rolled back as a scroll,
The trumpet shall sound and the Lord shall descend;
Even so it is well with my soul.[3]

(LSB 763)

Spafford didn't pen these words at his grand family estate with the percussion of giggles and pattering feet of young children. Yet he writes about the whispers of peace, of his hope and anticipation, in one of his darkest and most devastating moments—when nothing in this world would be enough to console him. Is it well with his soul, really?

I believe that as we face the tension between the ways this world falls short and the peace that goes beyond logic and explanation, we experience the living water that Jesus promises. Maybe, along with his peace, Spafford felt utterly wrecked. Perhaps in his darkest moments, he released sobs that sounded more like an untamed animal than a grieving man, his pain too great to form into words. I also believe that in those quiet mo-

---

3   Horatio Spafford. "It Is Well with My Soul." https://library.timelesstruths.org/mu   sic/
It_Is_Well_with_My_Soul/. Accessed April 27, 2020.

ments as he sailed over the ocean grave of his four girls, with waves as white noise and the forward movement of the ship rocking his weary body, Horatio Spafford experienced a peace and a hope that is not of this world. I believe that in those moments, his faith in the Savior was more than enough.

I cannot fathom losing my children, but I can relate to peace and stillness in a time of trouble. When my daughter was one, she began experiencing a string of random symptoms that were confusing and seemingly unrelated. Her face broke out in painful sores, and she wouldn't let me brush her teeth; each time I tried, her gums bled. She'd crawl into bed with us at night and thrash and moan, unable to get comfortable. We went to several pediatricians and specialists who tried to diagnose her. We tried topical creams and oral antibiotics. Nothing relieved her raw face and restless nights. After several weeks, we took her to a pediatric dermatologist who suggested a possible diagnosis, but it was not one we wanted to hear. One week later, our doctor confirmed that Elyse had a rare autoimmune disease called Juvenile Dermatomyositis (JDM). The autoimmune system attacks the skin and muscles of the body, causing muscle weakness, sores, rash, and pain. A week after that, I carried my daughter's crumpled form into the emergency room. She could no longer walk and was too weak even to lift her head. They admitted her to begin an intensive treatment that involved IVIG blood infusions, methotrexate injections, steroids, and other medications. Prayers covered us from our church members and from people across the country as we held our breath and waited.

For the two years prior to this, I had been blogging to process and communicate my experiences with life and motherhood. Friends, church members, and blog followers all waited for updates on how Elyse was doing. For the first several days, I relied on others to spread the news on her progress, but finally, one quiet afternoon as my daughter slept, I tried to sum up all I was feeling and experiencing as I strung together these words:

> To friends we know, and friends who have been praying and following us from afar. I don't know what to say, but I want to share with you an update on how we are doing and to thank you for all your love and prayers.
>
> *This is what I know:*
>
> I know my heart aches as I watch my daughter crumple to the ground, her legs too weak to skip or twirl or run until she can't catch her breath.
>
> I know a mother shouldn't have to sing lullabies to calm her baby as she twists and wrestles to be free, tears pooling in the corners of her eyes as she's poked again and again.
>
> I know the mom in the crowded waiting room of the ER—with her head bowed over the sleeping pile of a sick child—belongs at home with her feet propped on a table, her son tucked under his Thomas Train comforter in his bed.
>
> I know I'm not alone in suffering. I know we can drink life only in a bittersweet cocktail of overflowing joy and aching emptiness.

But I know so much more.

I know I am blessed more than my words can ever express.

I know a daddy who pushes his baby around the hospital floors for hours on end, who wears an ash cross on his forehead, his eyes filled with tears, but his heart full of unwavering loyalty and trust. A husband who stays all night on half of a twin cot because he knows his wife needs him.

I know a doctor run ragged with slumped shoulders, walking home, used up and tired, whose hands have healed more lives than faces he can remember.

I know the warm blanket of peace wrapped around me amidst the chorus of children's cries and the dull ache of fear and uncertainty.

I know more food than my belly can hold, more love and prayers whispered than I can imagine, more kindness than I can repay.

I know when we're broken, the love that binds us back together makes us more complicated and more beautiful.

I know a little girl who can't walk but believes she can "fly" through the trees in a green plastic swing.

I know a little girl who will walk and skip and run again, with a life story that sings like a love song.

I know beauty and grace can exist even in the corner of

a hospital room as I'm lulled to sleep by the hum of IV monitors and the soft snores of my little girl.[4]

Her daddy pushed Elyse many laps around the hospital in a plastic red car with her IV pole attached to it. The day before she was released, Elyse walked around the corridor on her own two feet as the staff clapped.

As I write this, I am in my favorite corner of my local Starbucks, and my little girl is at preschool, running and jumping in puddles. It's nearly impossible to distinguish her from other children, aside from her bright pink hat adorned with an oversized bow that she wears every day. Children with JDM are more sensitive to the sun, and overexposure can cause a flare, but her hat has become part of who she is, and sunscreen has become her second skin. We keep her on a gluten-free diet, and she takes a weekly medication of methotrexate, which is a low dose of a chemotherapy drug, but we're talking about weaning her from that in the next couple of months. While JDM is a lifelong diagnosis, remission is looking more than possible for her in the near future.

I didn't know about these happy outcomes when I wrote the blog post above. We know some children who lost their lives to JDM and others who will never achieve remission or live pain-free again. But from the moment in the middle of the night when I left my husband home with our older daughter and rushed my little one to the ER, to holding her as they tried again and again to get an IV in her little arm, to waiting all night

---

4   Lindsay Hausch. "This is What I Know as a Result of My Daughter's Rare Disease." The Mighty. https://themighty.com/2017/08/what-i-know-as-a-result-of-juvenile-dermatomyositis/. Accessed September 30, 2019.

for test results, to bringing her home with a regimen of medications that made my head spin, I experienced God's peace. I could sing along with Horatio Spafford, "It is well with my soul," and mean it.

My experience was a place where I was not enough to comfort my child, where doctors had not enough answers, where medicine was not enough to offer relief, where it felt like the medical staff could never move fast enough to meet our needs—in this place of utter lack, I felt the fullness of the Holy Spirit. In that place of my utter need, God drew me close and comforted me, even though my questions were unanswered and the future was unknown.

I don't want you to read this and feel a disconnect in your own experiences. It is easy to write about our past experiences in a way that seems tidier, that is tied with the beautiful bow of hindsight. I assure you that this journey also involved many tears, sleepless nights, and heart cries to God. I remember one day, after we were home from the hospital and still learning to navigate our new reality, I collapsed to my knees and sobbed as I remembered Paul's promise in Romans: "the Spirit Himself intercedes for us with groanings too deep for words" when we don't know what to pray (Romans 8:26). Our struggle through Elyse's illness felt like the ebb and flow of now and not yet. As I reached for the hope of a brighter future, I held close the peace God provided moment by moment, like a candle in a dark room.

Now and not yet marks the in-between time, the time of growth, when the land looks bare—its seeds still hidden beneath the surface. The night seems too long, and frost still clings when the calendar marks spring. In these not-enough times, when redemption feels tenuous and hope feels uncertain, Jesus' living water comforts us most and strengthens us as we come to the end of our own limitations. In these vulnerable moments, we reach out for more of Him.

Here I want to introduce a word that may be familiar to some, but to others, it might sound like a lofty word I pulled from a book. In either case, stick with me as we unpack the word together: *sanctification.*

Sanctification is the process that the Holy Spirit works within us to make us more like Jesus through reading and hearing His Word and being in relationship with the Father. Martin Luther draws a perfect picture of this:

> This life therefore is not righteousness, but growth in righteousness, not health but healing, not being but becoming, not rest but exercise. We are not yet what we shall be, but we are growing toward it; the process is not yet finished, but it is going on. This is not the end, but it is the road. All does not yet gleam in glory, but all is being purified.[5]

A key word here is *process.* The Spirit's work in our hearts is always ongoing and not completed until we are in heaven. What this means for you and me is that the Holy Spirit goes about the work of forming and reshaping our hearts even as

5   "The Wisdom of Martin Luther in 12 Quotes," *Christian Today*, accessed April 28, 2020, https://www.christiantoday.com/article/let-us-drink-beer-the-wisdom-of-martin-luther-in-12-quotes/118288.htm/.

we face challenges that cause anxious thoughts and uncertainties. When we face tragedy that leaves our souls bankrupt, God somehow brings enough water to sustain us in that moment. As we encounter each new challenge, endure each new struggle, we can remember that it is another opportunity for the Spirit to increase our faith and build our character. This doesn't always lessen the pain in the moment, but it helps us to look to a future good and to be comforted by the Comforter.

I'm sure you can back this up with your own life experience. Think of your five most life-changing moments—moments so pivotal that they are woven into the fabric of your history. I bet there are some hardships on your list. Perhaps, tucked under the celebration of your wedding, is the loss of someone you love, or a strained relationship. Maybe between the birth of your babies is a miscarriage, fertility struggle, or crippling depression. Whatever milestones make up your most significant moments, they are experiences that are a blend of big emotions: bright joy, anticipation, fear, uncertainty, grief, and sadness.

From the highs of celebration and joy to the lows of suffering and mourning, every experience weaves the fabric of who God is shaping and forming us to be as He equips us to live in this world. Our struggles are the warp and weft of contrasts that create depth of character. Suffering sews us together in relationship with others as we share their pain.

God puts our lives back together in a patchwork of profound experiences. The losses that are too great to comprehend on this side of heaven and the loves and passions that feel like miracles are stitched into something complicated and beautiful that tells the story of our life. Living it is painful, tedious, and sometimes senseless, but in God's hands, it is a sight to behold. In His hands, our Creator's hands, it is a masterpiece.

When I am able to zoom out to a bigger God perspective, I find gratitude in the midst of hard things. Gratitude helps me flip the script, to sing a new song. The Holy Spirit moves me to see an ordinary Monday as another day of daily bread and my child's rare disease as a place for Him to shine His light.

Yes, God gives me enough: enough gifts, enough hope, enough healing, enough love for today. More than enough, even enough to give it away.

The anxious thoughts of not enough melt into praise as Jesus meets me at the well and draws me out of my shame and hopelessness, as His Spirit stirs within me and reminds me that the living water He provides is more than enough.

ENOUGH TO GROW

KEY THOUGHT: While our anxious thoughts will never go away, God uses our suffering to strengthen our faith and deepen our knowledge of Him, which means as we grow in our spiritual maturity, we also grow in our capacity to respond in faith to our anxious thoughts.

Verses for Reflection

Therefore, since we are surrounded by so great a cloud of witnesses, let us also lay aside every weight, and sin which clings so closely, and let us run with endurance the race that is set before us, looking to Jesus, the founder and perfecter of our faith, who for the joy that was set before Him endured the cross, despising the shame, and is seated at the right hand of the throne of God. (Hebrews 12:1–2)

For My thoughts are not your thoughts, neither are your ways My ways, declares the Lord. For as the heavens are higher than the earth, so are My ways higher than your ways and My thoughts than your thoughts. (Isaiah 55:8–9)

Open Your Bible

Read Acts 2:14–41.

Questions to Consider

1. In Hebrews 12, Paul describes Jesus as "the founder and perfecter of our faith." What does he mean? How have you experienced this to be true in your faith?

    _____

    _____

    _____

    _____

    _____

2. We read in Isaiah 55, "So are My ways higher than your ways." How does that help you see your current life situation from a bigger perspective?

    _____

    _____

    _____

    _____

    _____

3. Lindsay talks about the word *sanctification*. What does it mean? Why is it important in our journey as believers?

    _____

    _____

    _____

    _____

    _____

4. Have you experienced a place of "not enough" that has resulted in a deeper relationship with God and others?

_____

_____

_____

_____

5. In Acts 2, we see the disciple Peter moving from denying Jesus to proclaiming who He is with boldness and conviction. How did this change occur?

_____

_____

_____

_____

_____

6. As you have matured spiritually, have you also seen a growth in your ability to cope with anxious thoughts? How or how not?

_____

_____

_____

_____

_____

Activity

God instructs the Israelites to remember and record the ways
He provided for them in their moments of need. Make a record
of a moment in your life when God provided for you in difficult circumstances. Describe how it has strengthened you for
future struggles.

_____

_____

_____

_____

_____

_____

_____

_____

CHAPTER 6

WHEN WE PRAY

John DeVries in his book *Why Pray?* illustrates prayer as a child flying a kite. The child does the work of stepping outside with kite in hand and lifting it into the wind, but he cannot make it fly.[6]

When we try to live without reliance on God in prayer, we're like the boy who runs in circles trying to keep the kite in the sky through his own activity. In prayer, God supplies the wind that gives our kite flying power. Whenever I catch myself running in circles of activity or whenever my mind spins in circles of anxious thoughts, I picture the boy huffing and puffing to make his kite fly on a windless day. Now, don't get me wrong. I've gone days, weeks, months, even years when I run in fretful circles, trying to keep my life aloft by my own effort and activity. But again and again, as I reach the end of my own strength, God reminds me of the power of relationship with Him in prayer.

PRAYER IS HOLDING HANDS WITH GOD

I don't know the exact moment when my marriage with Nathan went from honeymoon to hard work. The first couple of

6   John Devries. *Why Pray.* Grand Rapids, MI: Mission India, 2005, pp.67-78.

years of wedded bliss weren't easy as far as circumstances. Our actual honeymoon was a cross-country move from San Diego, where I'd been living, to St. Louis, where Nathan was finishing his last year of seminary. Six months later, we were off to northern Arizona to serve at our very first church. Homesickness and navigating a new community and new responsibilities took a toll on us both, but fueled by the love and excitement of being newlyweds, we pushed through. Two years later, when I became pregnant, however, escalating hormones, the isolation of where we lived, and a sudden job loss all sent me into an emotional spiral. Nathan, weighed down by his own stress and struggles, felt emotionally unavailable to me.

In our naivete, we thought some time apart would help us sort out our feelings. We decided that I would return to my parents' house, seven hours away, for two weeks to give us both space to breathe and work through our feelings. Looking at it now, I believe this was a terrible idea, but young and dumb, it was the best we could come up with. Although it wasn't a solution, it felt like something we could do to disrupt the cycle of hurt and misunderstanding that had crept into our lives and repatterned our days into a confusing and unrecognizable blur.

At our reunion, hope morphed into disappointment. After two weeks apart, Nathan came to stay at my parents' house for a long weekend before we would return home together. The tension between us had thickened into a mortar that bonded bricks of resentment and bitterness. We loved each other, but we didn't know how to communicate through the wall of hurt between us.

One morning, we drove to the coast to spend the day to-gether, but the silence in the car was poignant, no longer punc-tuated by jokes, stories, and laughter. Nathan pulled over and punched a new address into the navigation on his phone. No salty air and sandy toes; instead, we went to the church of an old friend, Eric, who volunteered to sit with us in this moment of crisis.

At the beginning of our time together, the first thing Eric asked us to do was hold hands.

Are you kidding me? I didn't even want to look at my hus-band, let alone hold hands with him. But in a smug display of effort, I offered my hand.

Nathan reached and wrapped his rough, warm hand around mine. We were aloof and disconnected, but this one touch point, our fingers intertwined, sighed of our longing for our hearts to mingle and twist together again—an impossibility in that moment, but a promise that each of us would try.

I held his hand through the confounding blend of resent-ment and numbness that made my skin electric, my limbs slow and dumb. I held his hand as hurt swelled in my chest and be-came needles of tears behind my tired eyes. Fat drops rolled down my face as words spilled out in incoherent sobs. And I held his hand.

Pastor Eric taught me a lot that day. The kind of learning that stings your throat like hot hearty broth and strengthens your bones. It was a lesson of moving in the world with more self-awareness and self-acceptance. He offered me the grace

I needed to see myself with painful clarity and the hope that could thaw and remold my cold, hard heart. Pastor Eric helped me to see that I was doing the impossible and frustrating work of trying to change my husband, when the only heart I could work on was my own. And in that painful process, I could hold Nathan's hand and wait and trust that he would also open himself up and allow God's Spirit to perform surgery on his own calloused heart. The first step, for us, was to link hands and stand firm in the sacred ground of our marriage vows, even when circumstances and emotions goaded us to let go and walk away. Pastor Eric was not only teaching me a new posture in our marriage but also a new posture in my faith.

Like the healing I experienced as I held my husband's hand, prayer is our way to hold hands with the Father as we stand on the security of our faith through the Spirit and our forgiveness through Jesus' work on the cross. When we come to God in prayer, we don't have to feel His closeness to know that He draws close. We don't need to use our emotions as the barometer of His love and faithfulness to us. Certainly, those feelings, the warmth of the Spirit in our midst, can be a thrill like no other. Yet, like a husband and wife are bound together by their marriage vows, God's love and promise are bound to us in Jesus, who secured us by His new covenant (see Luke 22:20).

I have learned to reach out and hold hands with Nathan, even when circumstances and my emotions draw me away. It isn't always easy to return to this place, but I do it, abiding in our marriage, a fortress when the storms rage within us and against each other.

God is that shelter for us. In Isaiah, He promises, "For I, the Lord your God, hold your right hand; it is I who say to you, 'Fear not, I am the one who helps you'" (Isaiah 41:13). As we hold hands with God, remaining connected to Him in prayer, He comforts us, guides us, helps us. As we reach out to Him in prayer, we remember that we are loved unconditionally and that His love shapes our identity. We are created in God's own image, like two hands that are mirror images of each other, our hand enfolded perfectly into God's. We are created for that purpose. But unlike any other relationship, God's hand is always reaching out for ours, ready, available, patiently waiting.

Life's trials can leave us on our knees; we can take the posture of prayer or the posture of defeat. On our knees, we can reach up and grab hold of God's hand as we remember our reliance on Him. In the swirl of hurt and anxious thoughts, we return to God's promise to help us as we hold hands with Him in prayer.

GOD BENDS TO LISTEN

Prayer anchors us to God's abiding love for us. When we crave His closeness, when we feel lost, isolated, and wave-tossed, our hearts bruised by life's storms, prayer is the distress signal. The Bible reminds us of God's love for us and His posture toward us. In Psalm 116, David celebrates that God hears his cries for help, that God "inclined His ear" to him, bringing to mind the image of a parent getting at a child's level to hear their little one's whispers:

I love the Lord, because He has heard

> my voice and my pleas for mercy.
> Because He inclined His ear to me,
>> therefore I will call on Him as long as I live.
>
> The snares of death encompassed me;
>> the pangs of Sheol laid hold on me;
>> I suffered distress and anguish.
> Then I called on the name of the Lord:
> "O Lord, I pray, deliver my soul!"
>
> Gracious is the Lord, and righteous;
>> our God is merciful.
>
> (Psalm 116:1–5)

I think of when one of my children is hurt or upset. I hear her cries and rush to be near her. I crouch down and pull him into my arms and kiss his tear-streaked face. Then, I look into his or her eyes and ask in rapt attention, "What's wrong? Why are you upset?" I not only listen but I let each word sink in as my heart feels the sting of his pain, fear, or disappointment. My closeness and attention give her courage to tell me all the heavy hurts on her heart and emboldens her to speak the fears that make her feel isolated and alone.

In the Old Testament, God describes His love for the Israelites like a mother's love. God promises:

> As one whom his mother comforts,
>> so I will comfort you.
>
> (Isaiah 66:13)

He promises to remember them:

Can a woman forget her nursing child, that she
should have no compassion on the son of her womb?
Even these may forget, yet I will not forget you.

(Isaiah 49:15)

Time after time in the New Testament, we see Jesus' nurtur-
ing love in His tender compassion and care for the people He
encounters, in the gentle way He listens, and in the gracious
way He speaks. And in His perfect sacrifice on the cross, Jesus
makes love complete.

The cross and the empty tomb are where we see proof of
God's power to heal and restore our broken hearts. As we rest
in this knowledge of who God is and what He has done for us,
we are emboldened to come to Him in prayer and to rely on the
vows He has made and already fulfilled for us.

PRAYER STARTS NOW

These illustrations preach beautifully, but they haven't an-
swered the practical question: how does prayer help me in the
midst of my anxieties and distractions? I hope you have a Pastor Eric in your life who will make time to be with you in your
crisis and remind you how to respond in faith. I encourage you
to identify people who will listen and point you to God's promises. Finding these people is a wise step to take before a storm
hits. This book also can be a reminder of our ultimate source
of hope and an encouragement to hold God's hand in prayer.

A daily rhythm of time in God's Word and in prayer is a way to
abide in God. As we do these things, He rearranges our hearts
and aligns them with His. This is a way to soften and prepare

for the storms that test our hearts and our faith. For me, there are days when this happens over coffee at the breakfast table with kids chomping down their bananas, chatting and clambering for my attention. Sometimes, this is all that my season of life can accommodate, and so I take what I can get. I've learned that waiting for the "best" time for daily devotions means they don't happen.

This morning routine is similar to the "dates" I have with my husband. Usually, these are simply a quick lunch when our older kids are in school or time together in the backyard over beer and a bonfire after the children have gone to bed. Have you used the same kind of flexibility spend time with the people you love and want a relationship with? What about your time with God? Imagine what your imperfect dates with God could look like. Then think about the small, simple—yet significant—shifts you can make to meet with God in your everyday life.

I don't know about you, but the longer I go not responding to a friend's message, well, the longer I go not responding to a friend's message. Hours to days, days to weeks, and so on, until before I know it, I haven't responded at all, and a once-familiar friendship can feel distant and awkward. Then I feel like I can't expect that friend to be there for me in the same way, as if I have to make an effort to earn back her love and trust. This has also happened in my relationship with God. After weeks of silence on my end, I feel the urge to strike up a conversation. "Umm. Hey, God. So, it's me. I know it's been a while. I know I haven't even earned the right to ask, cuz . . . well . . . I haven't been a good Christian, but do you think You could listen and hear this one little prayer?"

Have you also imagined God as a flaky friend in the sky that you need to persuade to give you time, attention, and affection? Your intellect may know that God doesn't operate like this, but there is still a flashing thought or the caution sign of guilt that causes you to pause before you pray.

I want to assure you of this right now: God is here, He is waiting, and He welcomes His wandering children with a warm embrace. Do not let your own uncertainty and insecurity distance you from the Father's love, which is always there for you. Do not let the evil one convince you that you aren't good enough for God to listen to.

This "right now prayer" can take the form of long conversation, or it can be a simple cry that acknowledges your need for Him.

A prayer can be as simple as turning our hearts to God as we recognize that we can't do this life without Him. "Lord, save me," Peter cried out to Jesus, who "immediately reached out His hand and took hold of him" (Matthew 14:30–31). Notice that Jesus was right there with Peter, watching and waiting for Peter to call out to Him. This account shows us that we, too, can cry out in utter vulnerability and need, and that God doesn't hesitate to meet us. He is just as real and just as present for us as He was for Peter.

My prayer for you and me is that we never let guilt or doubt come between us and God, that we don't let it keep us from reaching for His hand. God doesn't care about our fancy words or Bible knowledge when we turn our hearts to Him. This account in Matthew teaches us that Jesus Himself meets us in the storm—whether it's a storm that threatens the foundation of our lives or a worry that steals our calm. "Lord, save me." Some call this an arrow prayer, and it is a simple way to reorient our hearts toward Jesus as we look to Him for help.

We don't need to tiptoe into prayer as we perform the awkward dance of introducing ourselves or appearing wiser and more capable than we really are. We can rest in the knowledge that we are already fully known and fully loved by God. When we pray, we change course out of our spiral of anxieties, and God reaches down and pulls us out of the dark depths into which we are sinking.

As we shift our attention from inward to upward, God gives us renewed purpose and propels us into relationship with others. More, as we pray over the things that burden our hearts, we can trust that He not only hears and responds to our prayers but He also works in our hearts as we learn to see the world and respond to it differently.

Later that day when God led Nathan and me to Pastor Eric, his wife, Sara, laid hands on my "Bree-filled belly" (our older daughter), and the two of them prayed over us. They prayed for a hope and a future in our marriage, for our family, and for our ministry. We prayed and linked hands. We prayed with a cloud of witnesses. That day, they lifted up my arms when I was too weak. And God heard.

We pray with the hope of effecting change in our world and

circumstances. But it may be that the biggest change is hap-pening in our hearts. Prayer is a process where we loosen our grip on our own agendas and attitudes and seek for God's will and power to be unleashed in our lives. We go from dark spiral to somewhere that's worth going. The Holy Spirit leads us to a better understanding of how God sees us and knows us and to an enriched perspective of how we see and know Him. Prayer isn't an assignment we complete just to get points, nor is it req-uisite time with God that we do like a routine checkup. To be sure, it takes discipline and effort to show up again and again. But as we spill our hearts to God, we open ourselves up to His transforming power.

I hope this chapter encourages you to see that above ev-erything else, prayer is about relationship with God, who re-minds us who we are and empowers us to rely more fully upon who He is.

Maybe you already have a daily prayer routine. Or perhaps you feel the distance of guilt because you have drifted. Maybe you have never had a relationship like this with God, or you doubt His existence. Wherever you are, be assured that God's care for you and response to you does not depend on your ef-forts. You can cry out to God in prayer and trust that He bends down to listen. God wants to draw near, to meet us, to listen to our hurts, our doubts, and our fears. Regardless of the storm you are in right now, call out to Him. Set aside time to meet your heavenly Father one-on-one in prayer. Reach for His hand, even as hurt and doubt surge through you. Receive His love and His presence. He's there for you.

WHEN WE PRAY

KEY THOUGHT: Prayer is a transformative relationship with God as we not only bring our anxious thoughts and needs to Him but also allow Him to enter and rearrange our perspectives, our hearts, and our lives.

Verses for Reflection

But when you pray, go into your room and shut the door and pray to your Father who is in secret. And your Father who sees in secret will reward you. And when you pray, do not heap up empty phrases as the Gentiles do, for they think that they will be heard for their many words. Do not be like them, for your Father knows what you need before you ask Him. (Matthew 6:6–8)

Oh give thanks to the Lord; call upon His name; make known His deeds among the peoples! Sing to Him, sing praises to Him; tell of all His wondrous works! Glory in His holy name; let the hearts of those who seek the Lord rejoice! Seek the Lord and His strength; seek His presence continually! (1 Chronicles 16:8–11)

Open Your Bible

Read Ephesians 6:10–20.

Questions to Consider

1. Lindsay describes prayer as a relationship. Is this how you have thought about and experienced prayer? Why or why not?

_____

_____

_____

_____

_____

2. How are you holding hands with God through prayer? Does Lindsay's perspective invite you to reevaluate any aspect of your prayer life?

_____

_____

_____

_____

_____

3. Matthew 6:6–8 gives practical teaching on how we should pray. What are the things that grab your attention? Why do you think they are important?

_____

_____

_____

_____

_____

4. 1 Chronicles 16:8–11 suggests several ways that we can engage with God. What are they? How can they be an important part of prayer?

_____

_____

_____

_____

_____

5. In Ephesians, Paul highlights a spiritual battle where prayer is a key and effective tool. How can this knowledge influence your approach to prayer?

_____

_____

_____

_____

_____

6. Does prayer help you address your anxious thoughts? How?

_____

_____

_____

_____

Activity

A prayer journal can be a helpful way to pay closer attention to our prayers and the way we see God at work in them. Journaling our prayers is an exercise that can help us to physically release the burdens from our hearts onto pen and paper. Consider beginning a prayer journal or using the space below to write a prayer to God about something that is causing you anxiety.

_____

_____

_____

_____

_____

_____

PART II

THE HEART OF COMMUNITY

(IN)

CHAPTER 7

YOUR INNER CIRCLE

Five of us sat silently around a bowl of snack mix, open Bibles on our laps, as suppressed fear flashed across our faces. I looked from woman to woman, pleading with my eyes for someone to say something that would shatter the tension and instantly transform us into close friends. My brain was desperately devising something interesting to say; simultaneously, my eyes scanned the room for the easiest escape route.

It was the first time we met as a "life group," a small group of people who agree to meet regularly to study the Bible, pray, and enjoy one another's company. In the church, life groups can be considered a formula for spiritual growth and meaningful relationships. But for introverts and socially awkward people like me, getting to know a new group of people can be a cause for anxiety and self-loathing. But there I was anyway, in a circle with four other women, placated by finger food and armed with my Bible. The leader asked questions, but the room stayed silent.

I don't do exaggerated silence well. Something primal in me needs to say something, anything. I tried counting to five.

Silence, still. Finally, unable to help myself, I spoke. Then I didn't stop speaking. Meanwhile, my mind raced anxiously with all the ways I was making a total fool of myself. I feared the terrible things they could be thinking about me, but my words continued to spill awkwardly from my mouth as if they were mortar to form our group into something safe and solid.

Nathan and I had moved to the community five months earlier, so I was still figuring out who I was in this new place. The weekend before, three of my closest friends had come for a visit. Our love for one another filled us like the hot coffee in our mugs, and laughter spilled over. I had met with these ladies week after week for more than a year to study God's Word and share together the good, the bad, and the hard experiences of life. We had emerged on the other side as sisters. After a weekend of sweet belonging, I said a hard good-bye and now sat in a new living room, looked into four new faces, and faced the new challenge to form new friendships.

Finally, another woman, sensing the group's unease, suggested we go around the group and share our week's highs and lows—things that were going well and not so well in our lives. Her suggestion gave the group permission to relax a little, and I heard everyone release a collective sigh of relief.

When it was my turn, I drew in my breath as tears threatened. Did I play it safe with an easy answer, or did I reach deep inside and reveal the truth that was my heart pain? I did both. I shared my high, which was the joy and ease of spending two days with dear friends, and my low, which was the fatigue and anxiousness of my new reality. In a new town, church, and community, I lived with the constant tension of new relationships. And I felt exhausted and beaten up by my negative thinking, which questioned and critiqued my performance in every social interaction. I was tired and disillusioned—yet I longed to forge formative friendships that would lay the foundation for belonging in this new community.

After I spoke, they nodded. "You're not alone," one said. Another agreed, "I still question where I belong sometimes." The room transformed into a confessional as I looked at damp eyes and heard a chorus of whispers, "me too." We weren't there yet, I knew. It would take time for our group to find an easy rhythm, time to establish trust and love for one another that would form the foundation of our life group. But we'd broken ground.

What I realized that day is that we never actually arrive at a final destination when it comes to our relationships. The very nature of relationship is that it challenges us to be vulnerable. As we offer ourselves in relationship, we ask again and again, "Do you love me as I am?" "Will you love me, even if . . .?" Doing life with other people means a constant tug-of-war between our desire to be known and our fear of being exposed. But as we push through, we encounter the sweet shelter of love and acceptance. When we find our inner circle of people who know us and love us, our anxieties are quieted with nods of understanding, if only for a moment.

WORTHY

So let's express the obvious truth: getting to know people makes me anxious. Perhaps entering new relationships makes you a little anxious too. You love having a close circle of friends you can trust, but getting there means combating pesky self-doubt and inconvenient anxious questions: "Did I say the wrong thing?" or "What is she really thinking?" The reality is that finding an inner circle of friends takes exposure, tension, and doubt, and the process is never complete. As we intentionally do life together and let ourselves be seen, we expose our hearts to one another, with all the beauty, passion, insecurity, and imperfection therein. We learn the good and the bad of us in equal measure.

Living in community with others exposes us to hurt, heartache, and a chorus of anxious thoughts that wake us at three in the morning. But with community comes the incredible feeling of being understood, being loved despite our shortcomings, and being forgiven for all the ways we don't measure up. The very place we face our greatest weakness and vulnerability is the same place we find love, connection, and meaning in our relationships. This sweet belonging keeps us coming back and giving of ourselves. But sometimes, we let anxious thoughts have the last say, looping in our heads, taunting us, and tempting us to hold back, withdraw, and even isolate ourselves from the community.

As we've talked about before, there is no one solution that will fell the grizzly giant of anxious thoughts in any facet of our lives, including our relationships. This means we need to turn again and again to our Father and remember our identity in Him. My anxious thoughts, self-doubt, and insecurity don't have the last say. When I feel berated by a barrage of self-criticism, I look to God's truth to reset my heart. The One who formed me and knows my every thought has the final word. I cannot answer my own heart's accusations, but God's love answers for me. The apostle Peter reminds us that because Jesus lived, died, and rose for us, we not only belong but we are also God's chosen:

> But you are a chosen race, a royal priesthood, a holy
> nation, a people for His own possession, that you
> may proclaim the excellencies of Him who called you
> out of darkness into His marvelous light.
>
> (1 Peter 2:9)

Peter reminds us that we are worthy because of Jesus' love for us. Our God bridged the gap between His divinity and our humanity through Jesus. Jesus humbled Himself and came into a sin-darkened, desperate world to offer grace that embraces us where we are and brings us "into His marvelous light." Jesus extends a love and belonging for which we don't save up, clean up, or try to prove our worth.

I hear this with my ears, but I struggle to let this truth sink into my heart and change me. That is because, despite this unabashed love, Satan tries to plant a seed of doubt and shame in me just as he did with Adam and Eve in the Garden of Eden.

We know from the creation account in Genesis that God gave Adam and Eve good gifts, providing for them in every way. When He told them not to eat from one tree, the "tree of the knowledge of good and evil," He gave them accountability, responsibility, and personal choice. If they trust and rely on God, they will enjoy a perfect relationship with Him. But that didn't happen. They broke the trust. Eve even questioned if God really wanted what was best for her or if He was withholding something. She "took of its fruit and ate, and she also gave some to her husband who was with her, and he ate" (Genesis 3:6). Their new knowledge filled them with shame to be in God's presence:

> And they heard the sound of the Lord God walking in the garden in the cool of the day, and the man and his wife hid themselves from the presence of the Lord God among the trees of the garden.
>
> (Genesis 3:8)

Instead of coming when God calls, we, like Adam and Eve, feel vulnerable and exposed. We want to hide, cover, and deny our sin. This shame not only invades our relationship with God but it also contaminates our relationships with others. God created us for relationship with Him and with one another, so we long to be known. Yet we inherited the burden of sin and are weak amid Satan's continuous assaults, so we search for a place to hide and conceal our true selves.

FINDING REAL

From my front door, you can see only the parts of my house that aren't lived in. Throw pillows are propped in the corners of the sofa. Visitors are welcomed by a row of enthusiastic faces and happy family milestones collected in picture frames on the mantel. I welcome guests with a warm "How are you?" and light conversation. Then, I say a casual goodbye and "Hope to see you soon."

But on the other side of the house, hidden from the front door, are the family room and kitchen—where our family lives our life. An empty yogurt cup with a spoon balanced inside sits abandoned on the kitchen table beside a stack of half-opened mail. The family room floor is littered with my girls' discarded footie pajamas and piles of picture books marked by a child's sticky fingers.

I don't let just anyone step inside my messy world. When I invite a friend over, I tidy the house a bit, vacuuming the crumbs and stowing the clutter in an effort to show a more polished version of myself. It is only when someone stays a while and looks closely that they see the bursting junk drawer or the crayon scribbles on the wall.

When I was a little girl, my mom bought paper dolls for me to enjoy during long road trips. I excitedly scanned the pages of delicate faces and elaborate clothing, awaiting the moment that we would pack into the car with our pillows and snacks and my mom would allow me to cut them out. But as I peeled out each doll and folded the clothes over their flimsy bodies, I began to feel disappointed. I couldn't run my fingers over their silky curls or feel the stiff texture of their tulle tutus between my thumb and forefinger. It felt as though I pretended to play with dolls rather than truly play with dolls. The paper dolls were a replica of the real thing; the real dolls were hidden.

As adults today, hiding is more subtle. We feel the same longing for something tangible and authentic, but we settle for a counterfeit version. The polite "How are you?" is usually met with a practiced "Fine." We vent about our disappointments and frustrations on social media for a quick like or comment rather than engage in face-to-face conversation that demands intimacy. In a culture of quick and easy, we settle for superficial relationships, but our souls know the difference.

Are there times when you feel unsatisfied with the quality of your relationships? Are you settling for an imitation of the real thing? Have you ever wondered what would happen if you tore down the divide between your messy real world and the facade of your public-facing side?

What if there was no divide between what we allow people to see and what we don't? When I feel the tension between who I present myself to be and who I feel I really am, I'm challenged to consider what could happen if I were confident enough to reveal the real me to others. What if I became the kind of friend who walked into your family room on a Tuesday afternoon, sat on your couch covered with dog hair, drank coffee from a chipped mug and . . . just . . . stayed a while?

We might both feel exposed and self-conscious at first, but so what? Would we feel understood? unburdened? If we sit through the anxious thoughts that come with first encounters, if we let them rush in and rush past as we push through to God's design for community, then maybe we can reach the place where love and connection become our focus. Then we would focus on the relationship itself instead of on our anxiety about being rejected or misunderstood.

Satan put distrust between God and man. At the evil one's prompting, Adam and Eve chose to seek their own wisdom over God's provision, and their relationship with their Creator was broken. Man could no longer live in God's perfect presence.

But God never stopped loving His people. Even in that terrible moment, He provided for them by giving them a promise. He led them out of situations that would destroy them and guided them to safety—again and again. Eventually, just as He had promised, He solved the problem of sin once and for all in the person of His Son. He entered the broken world in order to take on the punishment for all sin.

We know the rest of the story, of course. We can be assured that God continues to show us what love is, and in His perfect love, we don't need to hide or be ashamed:

> There is no fear in love, but perfect love casts out
> fear.
>
> (1 John 4:18)

From Jesus, we receive love that can drive away doubt, shame, hurt, insecurity, and whatever other serpents of distrust try to place themselves between us and God. Because "God shows His love for us in that while we were still sinners, Christ died for us" (Romans 5:8). We see perfect love and forgiveness displayed for us on a cross as a banner for our relationships with others. In the imperfect business of human relationships, we learn to choose love and forgiveness to reconcile ourselves to one another.

BUILDING BRIDGES

Many of us desire more depth in our relationships, but we

don't know how to get there. I wish I had a five-step plan for pushing through the anxious beginning of a new relationship to get to the place of deep connection. But I don't. What I do have is experience and wisdom from the Bible.

When it comes to engaging with others, we can dig our holes and hide in them, or we can push past our doubt, criticism, and insecurity and build bridges to them. Experience has taught me that I can't overcome the anxiety of engaging with new people by trying to streamline the relationship-building process. It's messy, it takes time, and sometimes, even after lots of effort, it just doesn't work.

Relationships are built bit by bit, conversation by conversation. The development of a friendship doesn't lie in one encounter; rather, it happens over time through the gradual trust, closeness, and confidence that accumulates in small deposits through conversations, over coffee, between appointments, scheduled and intentional activities, and unscheduled and meandering events. As I orient my mind to see relationship as a journey rather than a destination, I can ease and push through temporary anxiety and remember that each interaction is only one step in the journey of building a strong relationship.

I'm a sporadic journaler; I've kept one since high school. I crack it open to reflect and write only when there's something I want my future self to remember. As I go through the process of forming deeper relationships with the people in my new town, I found this entry from a few months ago to be helpful and perspective forming:

Getting ready to launch into my fourth major move in the span of ten years, I'm asking myself how I will do this one differently. This time, there is one important thing I want to keep in mind. Rather than over-analyzing each of my social interactions—what I said or could have said differently, if her sideways look was intentional, or what he really meant by that flippant remark—I want to have the perspective to see each exchange with the new people I encounter as an individual plank in the process of bridging myself in relationship to others, bit by bit, over time.

(June 11, 2019)

Reading this now, I see the bridge as a helpful image as I walk through the vulnerable process of finding a new community. A bridge helps me to envision drawing closer to the connection I desire and to accept the reality that I'm not there yet. To further this illustration, I consulted my trusted friend, the Internet, and keyed in "the process of building a bridge" because I haven't the vaguest idea of the actual process.

I found an article titled "Our Bridge Building Process Is as Simple as Building Blocks."[7] With two daughters and a couple of bins of blocks in our house, that headline is something I get. The article outlined the step-by-step process and emphasized the importance of following the steps in order. You can't throw out planks and hope they stick. The first step is the foundation, which is designed for the type of soil it is to be anchored in. The

---

7   "Our Bridge Building Process Is as Simple as Building Blocks," *U.S. Bridges*, accessed August 18, 2019, https://usbridge.com/our-bridge-building-process-is-as-simple-as-building-blocks/.

foundation determines the weight load a bridge can bear.

What is this solid foundation we need to support our relation- ships? Faith is the anchor and support for every relationship— faith that allows me to see myself properly so I can respond to others with clarity and confidence. Shared faith with others is a foundational story that is bigger than ourselves. When there is misunderstanding or conflict in our relationship with friends of faith, we can trust that just as God guides our heart to repen- tance and restoration, He is also guiding theirs. God is in the middle, forming our hearts and perspective toward one anoth- er, nudging us toward sacrifice and forgiveness.

Paul communicates this desire for Christian relationship in his Letter to the Church in Colossae, wanting "that their hearts may be encouraged, being knit together in love" (Colossians 2:2). Once an enemy of the Church, Paul knows the transfor- mative power of relationship through the redemption of Jesus. As Christians, we know the threads of faith that tie our hearts to one another and to eternity. God's love through Jesus is the thread that knits us together.

THE PROMISE OF "WITH"

God's love helps us to love one another more fully, but be- fore that happens, He gives us Himself. By His sacrifice on the cross and as He comes to us in the Lord's Supper, He ultimately offers us His love and wholeness in our relationship with Him.

In light of this bold and dangerous love, we are exposed. No longer naked and ashamed, we are fully seen, fully known, and fully loved.

We don't need to be mass-produced, false paper cutouts of Christians, but people He made us to be, real flesh and bone. God calls us to look plainly at our broken world and go about the mission of repairing it—to get dirt under our fingernails and work with simple things like seeds and soil, clean water, a warm jacket, a meal, and a chipped mug of coffee shared over a real conversation. He served us on the cross, He serves us in the Divine Service—and we then go out to serve others in His name and with His blessing.

A life lived in relationship with Jesus means we are constantly challenged to be pushed out of our comfort zones—to say the first "I'm sorry," to look someone in the eye when we'd rather look away, to stand shoulder to shoulder with people who make us feel uncomfortable or out of place. Relationships can offer us safety and belonging, but they can also challenge our beliefs, behaviors, and assumed norms.

When I read that God formed mankind in His image, I see the sea of spectacularly different people and a singular God, and I conclude that He must be spectacularly complex in character. He could have made carbon-copied people with one-track minds, but He gave us individual intellects and wills to choose. Instead of creating robots that think, look, and act alike, He created people to be unique and to have individual personalities. That means some people wage wars and others organize peace rallies; some throw strong words and others whisper encouragement. He created mankind to sharpen one another, to challenge one another, to love one another, and to celebrate one another's beautiful differences and similarities.

God created Eve in the garden because He said "it is not good that the man should be alone" (Genesis 2:18). We are called to offer one another the ministry of our presence, not to fix one another but to be with one another, "rejoice with those who rejoice" and "weep with those who weep" (Romans 12:15). As we share life together, in celebration and consolation, we point one another to God to fill our ultimate need for relationship.

As we receive this perfect love and belonging in an imperfect world, we are empowered to focus less on our own shortcomings and more on extending God's love and belonging to the people we come in contact with. When we shift our focus from wondering if we belong to extending belonging to others, our world expands as our inner circle grows.

Living in close relationship with others can be a source of anxiety, but God models community His perfect design for us. In the first chapter of Genesis, we meet God, whose very nature is communal in the form of the Trinity. The first verse and chapter of Genesis introduces *Elohîm*, the Hebrew word for God in the plural form, which is paired with the singular verb for "create," which is *bara*. This anomaly could appear to be a grammatical error, but it is actually an intentional statement about who our God is. Genesis paints a picture of God existing, in the beginning, as the triune Father, Son, and Holy Spirit. This holy huddle of three-in-one created the world. God Himself is community, relationship, and love. God models the power of community to us in Himself by His very existence.

The sin that entered our world in the Garden of Eden is bent on pulling us apart. It broke our relationship with God, the ultimate source of love and acceptance. This is why Jesus, whose name in Hebrew is *Immanuel*, meaning "God with us," came to live among His creation as a baby, utterly helpless and dependent on his mother's love and care. God the Son models to us reconciliation through relationship and displayed in weakness.

When we practice the imperfect art of relationships, we also come face-to-face with our own human weakness. But as we reveal our humanity to each other, we build compassion and learn to see the world from one another's shoes. Relationships we hold close are stretched as we acquire a bigger perspective of the world. We feel like we belong and are understood as we share our struggles with someone willing to listen. Yes, as Jesus comes to be with us, we learn that God's promise for healing our anxiousness in a four-letter word—"with." When someone is with us, it makes the struggle easier in this lifelong journey.

Like a mother who holds her child and whispers, "Shhh, I'm with you," after a nightmare, God hushes our hearts and reminds us that we are not alone. He offers us a circle of people to figure out life with. Best of all, He draws us close to Himself.

> The Lord your God is in your midst, a mighty one who
> will save; He will rejoice over you with gladness; He
> will quiet you by His love; He will exult over you with
> loud singing.
>
> (Zephaniah 3:17)

YOUR INNER CIRCLE

KEY THOUGHT: God not only encourages us but He also commands us to share our lives with others in relationship, where we can find a safe place to share anxious thoughts and receive encouragement and insight. At the same time, we find an even greater joy that pulls us out of our anxiousness and into community, and we extend that encouragement to others.

Verses for Reflection

Love is patient and kind; love does not envy or boast; it is not arrogant or rude. It does not insist on its own way; it is not irritable or resentful; it does not rejoice at wrongdoing, but rejoices with the truth. Love bears all things, believes all things, hopes all things, endures all things. (1 Corinthians 13:4–7)

Put on then, as God's chosen ones, holy and beloved, compassionate hearts, kindness, humility, meekness, and patience, bearing with one another and, if one has a complaint against another, forgiving each other; as the Lord has forgiven you, so you also must forgive. And above all these put on love, which binds everything together in perfect harmony. (Colossians 3:12–14)

Open Your Bible

Read Mark 3:31–35.

Questions to Consider

1. 1 Corinthians 13 and Colossians 3 are a picture of relationship that is inspiring and also a bit intimidating if we try to do it with our own strength. How does God equip us to live this way in relationship with others?

_____

_____

_____

_____

_____

2. As you consider "God with us" in the person of Jesus, how does it inform the way you are called to be with others in relationship?

_____

_____

_____

_____

_____

3. In Mark 3, Jesus proposes a different definition for who our family is. Have you found a family in Christ? How does your shared faith inform your friendship?

_____

_____

_____

_____

_____

4. If you feel disconnected or isolated, what is the first step you can take toward forming a community that can support you?

_____

_____

_____

_____

_____

5. Are your relationships a source of anxious thoughts? Are they also a source of comfort as you cope with anxieties?

_____

_____

_____

_____

_____

6. How does your faith help you to extend grace to yourself and others as you live in relationship in a sinful world?

_____

_____

_____

_____

_____

Activity

Identify a friend who encourages you in your faith. How can you invest in that relationship this week? Also, identify a person you know who needs encouragement. How can you come alongside her or him?

_____

_____

_____

_____

_____

_____

_____

CHAPTER 8

TIME TO CONNECT

As we explored in the last chapter, God designed us for community, to live in relationship with others. We cannot deny that we are biologically built for face-to-face interactions. Human connection is one of the gifts God gives us to help us face our anxious thoughts.

Too often, I let stress, technology, and to-dos hijack precious face-to-face time with the important people in my life. I answer emails over breakfast, scan Facebook while my husband drives, or let conversations with my kids get interrupted by the need to vacuum or put clothes in the dryer. Can you relate? Do you ever let your friend or family time get interrupted to answer a phone call? After an exhausting day, do you sit beside your loved one, but your eyes are trained on a mindless show? Lights go out, and your day felt full, but your heart feels disconnected from it all. Yes, too often I succumb to this version of life as I absentmindedly overlook some of my most basic human needs.

The sin cycle continues, and stress makes us hungry for relief. We may turn to alcohol or caffeine, to calorie-laden foods or the latest fad diet, to social media or a television show to dull the ache of our discontented heart. Too often, we turn to fast and easy things that temporarily satisfy rather than choose the hard work of relationships. In moderation, food, entertainment, and social media can be good things, but when we turn to them more often than face-to-face interaction, these coping behaviors morph into things that isolate us from the community and connection we desperately need.

In his book *The Relationship Cure,* Dr. John Gottman suggests that relationships are built by small interactions over time, or as he calls them, "bids for connection." After observing hundreds of married couples, Gottman concludes that strong relationships aren't formed by deep and meaningful conversations as psychologists once thought, but by the thousands of casual interactions that people share, day after day, week after week. This goes beyond marriage; such connections build the framework of every relationship, whether it's with a sister, co-worker, or close friend. Each bid for connection is an opportunity to strengthen, maintain, or damage the bond between people. In each interaction, we respond to each other in one of three ways:

1. **Turn toward.** The husband asks his wife if she made the coffee. She turns toward him when she playfully musses his hair and asks, "Don't I make the coffee for you every morning, dear?"

2. **Turn against.** Asked the same question by her husband, the wife could turn against him and say, "Yes, I made the coffee. I make it every day, and you never appreciate it."

3. **Turn away.** When her husband asks if she made the coffee, the wife could ignore him and continue looking at her
   phone or ask him another question like, "Did you buy milk
   yesterday?"

What is surprising is that Gottman found that turning away,
deflecting or ignoring the other person, is the most damaging
response. So damaging that, in his study, the married couples
that were the fastest to divorce were the ones where the partner's main response was to turn away.[8] Turning against, while
harmful, at least invites further conversation. However, over
time, as a person feels ignored and invalidated by the partner
who turns away, the relationship becomes not only disconnected but even unsafe because the partner feels ignored and dis-
missed.

Our relationships can be the safe shelter we turn toward
during the anxious storms in our lives, or they can be the very
sources of our anxiety. While most relationships do involve
some degree of conflict, repeatedly turning toward each other
in small, humble, and loving ways is how we build lasting relationships that can endure trials.

In a modern world, this is increasingly harder to live out.
Many homes have multiple screens and calendars full of ex-
tracurriculars. With ways to distract, entertain, and occupy our
time, we may unintentionally be turning away from those we
love most. After a long day of running here and there, I crave
rest and quiet. But rather than meaningful time with those I

---

8   John M. Gottman, PhD, *The Relationship Cure* (New York, NY: Three Rivers Press, 2001), 15–21.

love, I can choose the fast fix of a screen to scroll through my social media, to shop deals online, or binge-watch a baking show—but my soul craves something more.

While family vacations and date nights can be amazing gifts for relieving anxiety and building connection, mental wellness and healthy relationships are built on the touch points throughout everyday life as we respond to one another in love.

We choose connection when we give people priority over tasks. We offer the ministry of presence when we are not only physically present with others but are also emotionally and mentally present. While this behavior takes time and intentionality, our physical need for it is real. Human connection can actually lower levels of the stress hormone cortisol while increasing our body's production of oxytocin, know as the "love hormone" or the "cuddle hormone." Yes, culture may try to pile expectations upon us that stress us out and strain our relationships, but we can find rest for our anxious minds as we return to the community and connection for which God built us.

A NEW WAY TO KEEP TIME

I've had ample opportunity to put this into practice in real life as I serve alongside my husband in ministry. My husband, Nathan, operates on a different clock I cheekily call "Nathan time." He keeps time not by the minutes on his watch as many of us do but by the people who cross his path. If he needs to remember something, I don't remind him of the facts but of the person and conversation. This means that something as simple as buying a new barbecue grill means setting up a time to grab a beer with the salesman to talk about his work-life balance. School drop-off is a moment to counsel and encourage a dad who is going through a divorce. "Nathan time" means that I relinquish my task-driven agenda for the God-portunities to offer and receive the ministry of presence.

If this sounds easy, let's back up a minute. I will be the first to tell you that it's messy. Nathan and I have had to work to figure out that balance. He has learned that sometimes he needs to say no to people so he can show up for our family, get to the office on time, and complete necessary tasks of parish ministry. And I have had to learn to extend to him extra grace and extra time so he can continue to be the man who doesn't rush past the people in his path but pauses to have the conversations they need.

TIME FOR A MIRACLE

Nathan demonstrates a pace and purpose in his life that is led by the example of Jesus, whose ministry was recorded for us in accounts of His encounters with people. This is especially illustrated in Matthew 14, when Jesus feeds the five thousand. However, this story can lose context if we jump right into the middle of the miracle, so let's back up a little.

Earlier in the chapter, we learn that King Herod has beheaded John the Baptist. "[John's] disciples came and took the body and buried it, and they went and told Jesus." When Jesus learns what has happened to His cousin, "He withdrew from there in a boat to a desolate place by Himself." But the crowds "followed Him on foot from the towns" (14:12–13).

So now you see that Jesus has just learned of the brutal death of His close relative, His brother in ministry—someone He has known from the womb. Jesus had planned to have time alone to grieve, but the crowd has followed Him and gathered on the shore. Now He has a choice. Does He stick to His plan of time in solitude, or does He connect with the waiting crowd?

You, of course, know the answer, "When [Jesus] went ashore He saw a great crowd, and He had compassion on them and healed their sick" (Matthew 14:14).

Luke's account gives us another picture of how Jesus responds, saying, "He welcomed them and spoke to them of the kingdom of God" (Luke 9:11). Then, the part you're probably most familiar with—He feeds them! Yes, here Jesus lets relationship direct His plans. The crowd's interruption gives way to one of His greatest miracles and demonstrations of how He wants us to respond. While we can imagine that Jesus still grieved for His cousin, we also see how connection transforms His solitary experience into something that is shared and transformational. Jesus shows us how human connection can be a balm as we face devastating loss—and in that bare place, God our Father not only provides for us but "is able to do far more abundantly than all that we ask or think" (Ephesians 3:20).

MAKING TIME FOR KINGDOM WORK

Stories from Jesus' life are inspiring, but sometimes, they may feel a bit out of reach. How does this apply to how I respond to unexpected people and interruptions?

Let's take a moment to visualize this. How would you respond if some of your friends showed up at your house unexpectedly? Would you keep them at the door and tell them it's a school night? Would you stress because your house wasn't picked up? Or would you open the door wide, whip up a pot of spaghetti, and invite them to stay and chat late into the evening? I want to be the girl who is carefree, who always welcomes and feeds people. But that is not always my natural instinct. If I'm honest, I'd probably be putting out a bowl of trail mix and checking my watch every five minutes.

I could take a cue from Jesus and my husband.

If you're an introvert like me, the idea of inviting a crowd of people into your living room on a Thursday night does *not* sound like a way to overcome anxious thoughts. Rather, it is a recipe for a panic attack. I get it. Remember we're talking in the hypothetical here. You may not be the outgoing gal who hosts huge dinner parties. I'm right there with you. But it's always about context. We see Jesus living in the balance of prioritizing people while also choosing to spend time with His Father in prayer or face-to-face with His disciples. Many resources call this balance the up (connect with God), in (connect with friends of faith), and out (connect with your community) of a life of discipleship.

It's taken many years for me to understand myself as a person who functions better in smaller groups or one-on-one. If this sounds more like you, then perhaps following Jesus' example looks more like welcoming a friend who is going through a hard time into your messy kitchen to offer her a cup of microwaved coffee and a listening ear.

The ministry of presence is a gift we offer and receive as we show up for the people God places in front of us. This means quieting the buzz of busyness and anxiety's harsh whispers by remembering that God has things He wants to show us through the people He places around us.

CHOOSE TO FAIL WELL

For a busy mom, this can feel like a tug-of-war between offering my presence to people and actually getting anything done.

We can fall into the trap of thinking we need to stockpile time to engage with family in a meaningful way, in the meantime, keeping our heads down, and our hands busy as we rush to get all the to-dos crossed off the list. A completed list means, finally, the freedom to really enjoy and pay attention to the people you love. Yes, this is a lie we can all buy into.

For much of my life, I have believed that I can do it all and that getting it all done will make me happy. As my life has gotten fuller, it has felt like I am constantly bailing water out of a sinking boat. Now, with three children and a high-maintenance dog—that boat has officially sunk! Friends, it is mathematically and scientifically impossible for me to accomplish it all. Okay, I'm terrible at math and science, but trust me on this.

And do you know what? Coming to terms with this is possibly the best thing that has ever happened to me.

As I've lost my ability to keep up with my compulsion to be prepared, cleaned up, and ahead, I've had to learn more about relying on others and leaning into God for comfort. For a control freak like me, this feels like a free fall—scary, invigorating, and kind of like the first time I went on an upside-down roller coaster, almost melted into tears, and then threw my hands in the air and shouted, "Let's do that again!"

Don't worry, you don't have to love roller coasters—you just need to love your people enough to try something that's a little uncomfortable at first. Free falling as we loosen our grip on our day planner means we practice trust that it will eventually get done; trust that if it doesn't all get done, then life will go on; trust that God is good and our people are understanding.

In this exercise of letting go and trusting, the most marvelous thing happens: we find the joy of moment-to-moment connection. We realize that we were so consumed with the water in our boat that we forgot we could swim. With the boat sunk, we actually look around and see that we're not alone.

Connection has room to enter when we make it intentional. Meaningful conversation can happen when we focus less on our agenda and more on the person in front of us. Lived out, it looks like practicing more self-control, asking more questions, and offering fewer answers. It looks like softening our grip on life, letting go some of our compulsions, assumptions, and fears, and, like Jesus, having compassion on people.

This also means letting go of our need to be perfect.

I love vacuum lines on the carpet and the shine of just-polished furniture, but I love doing puzzles with my seven-year-old and taking after-dinner walks with my family more.

This means we have to choose the things we're going to

fail at. Maybe that's an unkempt yard, a few extra pounds, and furniture that gets dusted once a month whether it needs it or not. But when we prioritize people over perfection, we discover that time is too short to sacrifice opportunities to share life with people who matter.

"Shoulds" like "I should be thinner," "I should know how to do that," or "I should have more friends" inspire guilt and anxiety rather than compassion and connectedness. A wise counselor once told me, "Don't should on yourself." Well, that's one way to remember it! I encourage you to spend some time in prayer as you consider the things you're going to be bad at and the areas you want to prioritize. When "should" tries to enter, measure it against your priorities. Ask, "Is this something I really value?" If it is, rather than dwelling in guilt, schedule a time to process and reprioritize. If it isn't, let the guilt go. A friend offered me a way of talking about how I use my time that highlights what I'm presently making a priority. Rather than saying "I don't have time to exercise or (fill in the blank)," I can say "Exercise (or fill in the blank) is not a priority for me right now." Saying it this way can help us be honest and better evaluate what we are choosing to make time for and what we aren't prioritizing in our schedule.

Make a list of the things you give yourself permission to fail at and hold yourself to it. Here are the top three things I have chosen intentionally to fail at. I hope it helps inspire your own permission-to-fail list.

I CHOOSE TO FAIL AT THESE:

1. <u>DIY anything</u>: God bless the DIY people. I love their creativity and resourcefulness. But these things do not work out well for me, so I leave it to craftier folks and shell out money for their beautiful handiwork on Etsy. This means I generally avoid Pinterest and say no thanks to DIY valentines, art projects, home decorating, and Halloween costumes.

2. <u>Hard-core workout programs and diets</u>: Been there, tried that. A friend might have the best and greatest program— for her. For me, I'd rather invest my time and attention into other things, like reading in the morning, taking long walks, and making healthy meals for my family.

3. <u>Landscape and decor</u>: My house will never be featured in Better Homes & Gardens. My house is not the brightest on the block at Christmas, and we don't deck the halls for every single holiday. I love admiring other people's homes, but during this busy season with three young children, my home is not the place I choose to invest all my money or energy.

Make your own "I Choose to Fail At" list and embrace the time these failures give you to love others well.

I pray that as you make more time for those you love, your days feel less anxious and more purposeful. If you're like me, it might feel a little uncomfortable to not let your agenda have the final say when, for example, you are late arriving somewhere because a conversation was just too important to cut short. It might take extra self-control to linger at the dinner table to listen to your children talk rather than rush to get up and clean the kitchen. But when you push through the urge to be in control and let go, you might find that you feel less stressed and more connected, and maybe what you need most is to listen and be heard.

God has a gentle way of reminding us that there is a better way. He gives the example of Jesus so we can discover that one of the ways He helps us overcome anxious thoughts is human connection.

When I surrender my plans to Him, things don't always go the way I imagined—usually, they don't. But whatever the detour is, I know God has plans and purpose that will open my eyes to something more meaningful than my own narrow agenda. I also know He uses me to show up for others in an intentional way.

GOD'S ULTIMATE PRESENCE

This chapter wouldn't be complete without taking a dive back into the Old Testament to remember God Himself is different from false gods because He actually dwells with His people. When you spend time in God's Word, I encourage you to highlight every time God promises that He is with His people. Friends, let His promise soak in again and again and be amazed—you will find it repeated hundreds of times!

I often turn to Exodus 13 when I am anxious about unknown paths. Here, we read about the Israelites' treacherous journey out of Egypt and how God not only comes to be present with

His people but also goes before them and guides them,

> And the Lord went before them by day in a pillar of
> cloud to lead them along the way, and by night in a
> pillar of fire to give them light, that they might travel
> by day and by night. The pillar of cloud by day and
> the pillar of fire by night did not depart from before
> the people.
>
> (Exodus 13:21–22)

Read and remember that the God who guides us and invites us to connect boldly with others is nearby. He shows His radical love through His own presence with His people. Let Him draw you close now as you experience His love that makes you love boldly.

TIME TO CONNECT

KEY THOUGHT: God helps us overcome our anxiousness by inviting us to be present with the people He places us with. When we live a life that makes human connection the priority over our task list, we find opportunities to love others well and trust God to ultimately meet our needs.

Verses for Reflection

And when all the people saw the pillar of cloud standing at the entrance of the tent, all the people would rise up and worship, each at his tent door. Thus the Lord used to speak to Moses face to face, as a man speaks to his friend. (Exodus 33:10–11)

By this we know love, that He laid down His life for us, and we ought to lay down our lives for the brothers. But if anyone has the world's goods and sees his brother in need, yet closes his heart against him, how does God's love abide in him? Little children, let us not love in word or talk but in deed and in truth. (1 John 3:16–18)

Open Your Bible

Read Matthew 14:10–21.

Questions to Consider

1. As you read Exodus 33:10–11, what image comes to your mind? How do you envision the Lord speaking face-to-face as a friend?

   _____

   _____

   _____

   _____

   _____

2. How does this image help you to think about how you can connect with God? with others?

   1 John 3:16–18 is clear direction for how we should love others. What does that look like in your life today, and why is it important?

   _____

   _____

   _____

   _____

   _____

3. How can you offer more presence in your daily life?

   _____

   _____

   _____

   _____

   _____

TAKE HEART

4. Do you think this practice can help you cope with anxiety? Why or why not? Don't be afraid to be honest here.

_____

_____

_____

_____

_____

5. In Matthew, we see Jesus respond with compassion when He is met unexpectedly by a crowd. Does reading this make you think differently about how you can respond to others when their presence is unplanned?

_____

_____

_____

_____

_____

Activity

Create your own "I Choose to Fail At" list. How does intentionally failing help you release the pressure to keep up? How will you use that time differently?

_____

_____

_____

_____

_____

148

CHAPTER 9

LET'S FACE IT

Relationship and connection are good, but when it comes to doing life with others, there is one thing that is unavoidable in most relationships. If "conflict," comes to mind, then you know firsthand what I'm talking about. While relationships and community can help our anxious thoughts, they can also be the source of anxiety. I don't know about you, but when it comes to dealing with conflict, I get an *A*. And that *A* stands for avoidance. Yes, I am great at avoiding an uncomfortable situation, and I'm even better at getting anxious about it. However, when it comes to living in relationship with others, the Bible is pretty direct. There is no better substitute for face-to-face conversation.

John writes, "I would rather not use paper and ink. Instead I hope to come to you and talk face to face, so that our joy may be complete" (2 John 12). For John, a letter on paper, even one that is the inspired Word of God, does not substitute for a personal conversation.

This shakes me up a little. How often have I sent a text or an email to communicate a message that I could have said in person? When have I chosen just to drop something at someone's door rather than ring the doorbell and encounter them? I know I'm not the only one guilty of pretending not to notice someone I recognize when I'm out running errands because I'd rather not get caught up in a conversation right then. As an introvert, sometimes face-to-face time feels more like obligation and less like fun, but John puts it in a way that challenges me to reconsider.

Technology makes it easy to duck out of face-to-face conversation, replacing it with email, text messages, and social media. We can feel connected and caught up with our friends on Facebook or Instagram without seeing them in person. While social media can be a helpful tool for staying in touch or communicating information, it can also replace the time together that John emphasizes as essential. Certainly, John's words apply to his era, but they are also a lesson for us in our age of technology. Talking face-to-face is an essential element of human relationship.

LET'S TALK CONFLICT

John's desire to connect in person is not only important for sustaining relationships but it's also essential for moments of conflict when we need to have the hard conversations.

"Can we talk?" That three-word question is like a shot in the arm. It actually pains me. It courses cold through my body, ending with a full-body shudder and my eyes bulging out of my head. Then, I will usually feign casual detachment and mutter incoherently, "Definitely, maybe." Cough. "What's up?"

When direct contact is initiated, I'm usually not surprised. I've already felt the tension, maybe even heard murmurs. I've analyzed the way the conversation should go a thousand times in my mind. But the question "Can we talk?" sets the ball in motion.

Confronting an uncomfortable situation can be awkward and even painful. It can drag things into the open that we didn't know were hiding. It can drag things we've said or done into the light when we'd rather keep them in the dark. When we talk, we face our fears, our mistakes, and our hopes for the relationship. We expose the truth that we are vulnerable and flawed, and so is the other person. When we talk, we are challenged to stop pouting, ruminating, avoiding, and over-analyzing. We are challenged to confront the situation. We are challenged to utter big and sacred words: "I was wrong." "I forgive you." "You hurt me." "I'm sorry." "Can you forgive me?"

You may wonder how difficult conversations can be the way to overcome your anxious thoughts when facing the person you've been avoiding feels like facing a firing squad! Here is how it works. Sometimes, our anxious thoughts help us go to the place in our heart where things need to be set right. When we bring our anxious thoughts to God in prayer, we find peace to move past them, but sometimes, God challenges us to face them. The difficult conversation can be the antidote we need for peace and healing.

Finally, brothers, rejoice. Aim for restoration, comfort one another, agree with one another, live in peace;

and the God of love and peace will be with you.

(2 Corinthians 13:11)

WHERE TWO OR THREE ARE GATHERED

Christians often look to this particular verse from Matthew as a framework of how to approach disagreements among believers.

> If your brother sins against you, go and tell him his
> fault, between you and him alone. If he listens to you,
> you have gained your brother.

(Matthew 18:15)

God doesn't give us commands just to boss us around. (Okay, as a parent, I might be guilty of that terrible answer that sounds more like a power trip than productive advice: "Because I said so!") But we see throughout Scripture that God guides His people to do the things that will help them and that offer them peace. When we deal with anxiety-producing conflict the way Matthew advises, we don't see a magic spell for instant friendship. Rather, we see necessary groundwork for the hard work of healthy relationships.

Too often, Christians morph Matthew 18 into a rule without the grace it is wrapped in. God allows His people to offer His forgiveness to one another in relationship, which is good news! "Truly, I say to you, whatever you bind on earth shall be bound in heaven, and whatever you loose on earth shall be loosed in heaven" (Matthew 18:18). And more: Jesus promises to be there when people come together to have hard conversations, and

He offers grace. "For where two or three are gathered in My name, there am I among them" (Matthew 18:20).

I pray that the next time you read these verses, rather than seeing them as anxiety-producing, you see them as grace-giving. Matthew shows us how we can have restored relationships. Sometimes, that means we must do the hard work of being vulnerable and honest, of releasing our hurt and offering forgiveness, of coming face-to-face with the person who hurt us, of confessing and receiving forgiveness. But this hard work, this heart work, brings peace.

> Blessed are the peacemakers, for they shall be called [children] of God.
>
> (Matthew 5:9)

THE RISK OF TECHNOLOGY

In a predictable twist, man thinks he has a better solution: "God, why do I need 'go' and tell my brother when I can send an email or text or meme? Or maybe even a phone call or video chat? Or how about I avoid this uncomfortable conversation all together and just put it out there on social media?"

You see where this is going. The things humans have created to facilitate more connection are the very things that cause people to feel alone, misunderstood, and sometimes, ignored.

That said, if there is one thing the COVID-19 pandemic has shown us, it's that connecting with others via online applications and services and using social media platforms is better than no interaction at all. These technologies have not only helped people perform their jobs from home, but they have also been the only source of connection for many who were forced to shelter-in-place alone. Video chat apps allowed families to say good-bye to dying loved ones when being at their bedside wasn't an option.

In a world with endless online problem-solving opportunities at our fingertips—from shopping, to food delivery, to social connection—we must learn to balance these convenient tools in ways that are helpful and life-giving, while also continuing to turn to God's Word as the ultimate blueprint for our lives.

This means that while social media allows us to "unfriend" a person without ramifications, we are called to reconciliation by having those face-to-face conversations. When we handle conflict well, we actually avoid unnecessary stress and anxiety. We are accountable, but not only to ourselves. Whether or not the conversation results in a resolution, we can have peace that comes from knowing we honored God and the other person by how we handled the situation.

I am not a conflict expert or a trained therapist, but I can tell you that I have made every mistake when it comes to dealing with conflict. From the school of hard knocks, I have cobbled together a diagram to guide you when you are considering the best way to engage with someone.

You will see that the top of the pyramid is the most direct form of communication and the foundation of nearly every relationship: face-to-face communication. If possible, we should have difficult conversations face-to-face. If distance (or sheltering-in-place due to a global pandemic) is an issue, video chat is an option.

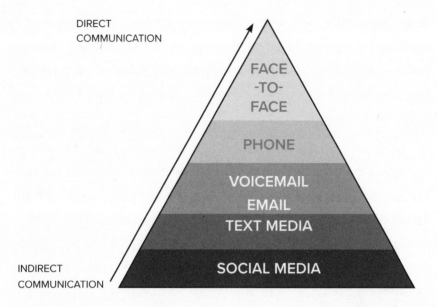

DIRECT
COMMUNICATION

INDIRECT
COMMUNICATION

FACE
-TO-
FACE

PHONE

VOICEMAIL
EMAIL
TEXT MEDIA

SOCIAL MEDIA

As we move to the bottom of the diagram, we see less direct forms of communication. The written word, in the form of an email, for example, can be a good way to process feelings and organize thoughts, but it may leave room for misunderstanding that can exacerbate the conflict. A text message, while tempting, eliminates tone and inflection and can cause greater confusion and hurt feelings. (Emojis are fine and fun in some contexts, but not in conflict resolution.)

Use the above pyramid to determine how you've responded to others, and consider how easy it is to say hurtful things when the communication is more distanced by technology.

When we publicly share our hurt, grievance, or annoyance with someone on social media, we deny them the opportunity to defend themselves, and we invite an audience that can take sides and pile on. I love Paul's teaching, "Do not let the sun go down on your anger, and give no opportunity to the devil"

(Ephesians 4:26–27). I have adopted another guideline that I created for myself: "Do not post on social media when feeling angry, needy, depressed, or emotionally unstable." And taking it a step further, I avoid social media altogether when I am in a negative headspace.

Social media is a fun platform for connecting, but it is also a breeding ground for hurt and misunderstanding and a source for anxiousness when misused. When in doubt, and even when not in doubt, talk face-to-face to address relationship conflicts. You will be gratified by this productive practice for overcoming anxious thoughts and doubts that arise in relationships. And if your friend listens to you, you will have deepened your friendship.

LOVE YOUR NEIGHBOR

When I was a child, I had to memorize and recite the Ten Commandments. Doing it by rote made them stale and flavorless on my lips—words I spoke without passion or real understanding. That is, until I was an adult and decided to read the Old Testament verses. When I read Leviticus, the command "love your neighbor" took on more than just meaning. It took the face of a person I knew I needed to talk to.

> You shall not hate your brother in your heart, but you shall reason frankly with your neighbor, lest you incur sin because of him. You shall not take vengeance or bear a grudge against the sons of your own people, but you shall love your neighbor as yourself: I am the Lord.
>
> (Leviticus 19:17–18)

Hate can hide in plain sight. I had held on to and ignored a grudge for so long that it had crawled into my heart and infected my thoughts. Consciously, I didn't think it was hate—more like jealousy, resentment, annoyance, and even apathy. But I had swallowed the hate with the lie that I couldn't confront it. I had swallowed hate whole and allowed it to poison my insides.

God encourages us to talk directly and right away with the person who offends us. It's a habit that, when put into practice, helps us to avoid the negative spiral of gossip, grudges, hurt, anger, and avoidance. While uncomfortable initially, this practice helps us avoid the anxiety caused by over-analyzing, misinterpreting, and judging others' intentions.

Paul advises us in Galatians that if anyone is caught doing something wrong (hurtful, annoying, unhelpful, destructive, or offensive), we should "restore him in a spirit of gentleness." But then he warns, "Keep watch on yourself, lest you too be tempted" (6:1).

When we avoid the hard conversations, we can get caught up in other ways of processing our hurt—such as anxious ruminating, judging others' intentions, or even gossiping—that can ultimately be harmful to ourselves, our relationships, and the other person's reputation. This is why the commandment to "love your neighbor as yourself" goes further than the five words we memorize in Sunday School. Loving as God commands means talking to our neighbor in order to avoid harmful reactions that can poison our thoughts and our hearts.

Sometimes, after talking with someone, we still don't reach the outcome we desire. There are people we must figure out how to have a relationship with: parents, siblings, in-laws, co-workers, and others in our church. In these instances, I focus on aiming for progress over perfection. Once we've had a face-to-face conversation, we can move forward with confidence that we have taken the right steps toward resolution, even if it isn't the perfect relationship we desire. There are, of course, people who are abusive or toxic that we must ultimately break ties with in order to keep a healthy mind and heart. Relationships are complicated, and anxiety caused by relationships is a very real and exhausting struggle. The most beneficial support I have received in this area was through meeting regularly with a therapist.

I finally talked to the person whom God had put on my heart when I read Leviticus, but it wasn't an automatic fix. It took time for our hearts to heal and for our relationship to return to a comfortable shape. While some relationships cannot be restored to what they once were, communication can help both sides forgive and move forward. "Can we talk?" isn't an easy question, but it's an opportunity that opens the door to healing as we seek to reconcile and embrace love.

COME TO THE TABLE

When it comes to mending relationships, I am definitely a work in progress. Running into someone who has hurt me is not at the top of my list of favorite activities. Clearly, Jesus has more to teach me. In Matthew 26, we get just one glimpse into Jesus' character in the face of disloyalty. It's easy to think of the Last Supper in the Upper Room as a *kumbaya* moment, but when we remember that Jesus already knows what is coming in the hours ahead, we understand that at this meal, Jesus has already forgiven the disciples for sins they have not yet committed against Him. Jesus knows that all His disciples will deny and abandon Him. He knows that Judas will betray Him and set in motion the horrible events that will lead to His death. And He still washes their feet and institutes the Sacrament of Holy Communion that invites them, and us, to receive His presence, body and blood, in the bread and wine of this precious meal that we still enjoy today.

LET'S FACE IT

KEY THOUGHT: As we live according to God's design of forgiveness, reconciliation, and honest communication, the Lord helps us to overcome the anxious thoughts that come as a result of relationship conflict.

Verses for Reflection

Finally, brothers, rejoice. Aim for restoration, comfort one another, agree with one another, live in peace; and the God of love and peace will be with you. (2 Corinthians 13:11)

Brothers, if anyone is caught in any transgression, you who are spiritual should restore him in a spirit of gentleness. Keep watch on yourself, lest you too be tempted. Bear one another's burdens, and so fulfill the law of Christ. (Galatians 6:1–2)

Open Your Bible

Read Matthew 18:15–17.

Questions to Consider

1. Second Corinthians 13:11 says to "aim for restoration."
   What does that mean? What does that looks like in a relationship?

   _____

   _____

   _____

   _____

   _____

2. Galatians 6:1 warns, "Keep watch on yourself, lest you too
   be tempted." What does this mean? Have you been tempted when dealing with conflict? Describe it. How can you
   follow Paul's caution?

   _____

   _____

   _____

   _____

   _____

3. Does conflict with others stir up anxious thoughts for you?
   Why or why not?

   _____

   _____

   _____

   _____

   _____

4. Matthew 18:15–17 offers a blueprint for how Christians
    should handle conflict. Have you practiced this in your
    relationships in the past? What good resulted from it?

    _____

    _____

    _____

    _____

    _____

5. As you read this chapter, did you feel convicted to initiate
    a conversation with someone or to release an old grudge?

    _____

    _____

    _____

    _____

    _____

Activity

In a quiet place, pray that God would guide you to live more
rightly in relationship with the people He has placed in your
life. As names or difficult situations pop into your mind, envision placing them in God's loving hands, and ask Him to give
you the ability to see the person or circumstance through His
eyes. Write how you felt God guiding you.

_____

_____

_____

_____

_____

PART III

THE HEART OF CALLING

(OUT)

CHAPTER 10

A MESSY MASTERPIECE

Here is a glimpse of things I needed in order to meet you here today:

1. **A (clean) public restroom.** Because nothing can be more distracting than a full bladder when a girl is trying to write.

2. **A big cup of dark roast with an ample splash of cream.** These days, with three kids, one an infant, I need a dose of alertness before I can form a coherent thought.

3. **A word document.** Full of fragmented thoughts and stories that I hope will come together into a message of hope and purpose.

4. **A messy heart.** Bursting with anticipation, confidence, anxiety, uncertainty, and hope that I pray will result in a chapter that explains my complicated journey to finding my calling as a mother, wife, writer, and woman of God.

This list illustrates that these chapters you have read weren't written in an easy stream of words. Rather, they have been collected in a process of wrestling, wondering, and walking through everyday life. It's easy to look at a finished book and forget that it is written word by word, like the drip, drip, drip of coffee brewing slowly in the strain of life experience.

As you read through the pages of this book, your own life unfolds moment by moment in a bright and confusing blend of beauty, struggle, and commonplace. In the swirl of a busy and ordinary life, it's easy to put calling on a shelf as something we will do someday. Someday, when the kids are grown, I'll write the book. Someday, when the bills are paid, I'll take the mission trip. Someday, when I earn the degree, I'll do the meaningful work I feel called to.

Do you find reasons that you can't do the great work you feel called to do? While you put your desires on hold, do you fret that maybe your passions and talents are fading from disuse? As women, we often feel anxiety and guilt for not living the life we feel called to, but when we do, we feel guilty for not fulfilling our responsibilities at home. This tug-of-war can leave our hearts tired and our souls disconnected from our everyday lives.

But something new can happen in your heart as you discover the mysteries of God that are tucked within this moment. When we shift our attention away from our own circumstances and abilities and toward God's blessings and opportunities, we can uncover the small ways God invites us to live out our calling today—even right now.

In Psalm 105, David reminds himself and others to "seek the Lord and His strength; seek His presence continually!" (v. 4). David demonstrates how to do that in the next verse: "Remember the wondrous works that He has done, His miracles, and the judgments He uttered" (v. 5). David, who has slain lions and bears, who defeated Goliath with a single blow, who was the chosen king of Israel and the man after God's heart, doesn't emphasize his own gifts or greatness in the Psalms. Rather, he consistently points to the ways, big and small, that God provides for him and his people.

David didn't write the Psalms for others; he wrote them for himself, because he needed these reminders in the tedium and struggle of his everyday life. He needed to remember that God was with him as he fled and hid from Saul. He needed to remember that God was at work in the everyday moments as he waited thirty years to take the throne of Israel, overlooked by his father, hunted like a criminal by his predecessor. David was a great man who endured the struggle of everyday life, but he returned to the path God was calling him to by continually remembering his great God. He sought God's strength and presence in every situation, when he was cold and shaking with fear, when he was hungry and alone, when his circumstances seemed impossible, when he was consumed by anxious thoughts of uncertainty.

When we try to turn our calling into something great that transcends our everyday realities, we may forget that God has placed us in this day, with these people, and in these circumstances for His purpose. Even if it feels scary and uncertain, tedious and ill-timed—even if it feels like a detour from our perfect plans.

What are the things you needed to meet me here in this moment? Did you need a steaming cup of tea or a heating pad for your sore back? Did you need a quiet house, scratching your toddler's back until he sank into the heavy breath of a nap? Maybe your list is intangible. You needed the resolve to release the guilt of taking a break from your list of tasks to sit and crack open to this page. Maybe this book is the very thing you hope will meet your needs now, because your heart is heavy with worry and you ache for relief.

You are not alone in this human experience of life being hard, in the feeling that sometimes you are in the middle of a detour from your real plans, or in the realization that life is not the great adventure you dreamed of as a kid. I am not writing to you now because I have it all figured out. I'm writing in the midst of a messy life, with tense relationships, health struggles, unexpected bills, and wrestling to understand the detours my own life has taken. But together with you, I seek to rest in the assurance that "where the Spirit of the Lord is, there is freedom" (2 Corinthians 3:17). This freedom isn't an escape hatch from the struggles and strains of life but a promise of His renewal in our everyday uncertainty and a promise of His ultimate restoration of our lives and world—our salvation through Jesus.

We receive this freedom as we read God's Word, as we pray, as we encourage one another, and as we read encouraging words from others. As the Spirit renews and releases us from the weight of this world, we are then freed to extend peace to others. We do it, not in grand displays, but wrapped within the simple sustenance of day-to-day needs. We walk the dog and talk to a neighbor about her garden, we feed the kids and talk to them about the importance of eating their vegetables, we kiss boo-boos, we encourage co-workers, we pray our way into sleep. Then we do it all over again the next day, and we trust all the while that as we plod forward faithfully, God will transform our small efforts into His mysterious grace. This daily struggle to give God our worries as we do the next right thing before us can be described in our culture by the lofty word *calling*.

It's easy to elevate the concept of calling, thinking it is something greater than the messy and mundane moments of everyday life. In reality, though, when we wrestle our desires in the grip of our anxiety, by acknowledging God's promise that He is with us and will accomplish His purposes through us, we come to an understanding that our calling can be unremarkable to us and still give glory to God.

CALLING IS A PROCESS

Do you see others living out their calling in their church, career, or family, and think that God has gifted and blessed them with more? More talent, more faith, more opportunity? It's easy to see the success of others and think they have it all figured out. When we look at the outcome and forget about the process, we neglect to see God's redeeming work in our lives and the lives of others. Focusing on the accomplishments of others can lead to anxious and confused thoughts about our own purpose and progress.

Calling can feel a lot like pressure. It can feel like a push to look better, be smarter, and achieve more. Too often, our culture pressures us to define from a young age what we want to be. For young adults, this push to define their calling can overwhelm and disorient. It can lead them to squeeze into plans for their future that don't suit them. We can take heart, knowing God is always going about the work of forming us, sometimes despite our own efforts of self-realization. Like Michelangelo sculpting his famous *David*, God goes about the work of carving and chiseling off the parts of us that don't belong, even when we are immature, insecure, or shortsighted in our own views of ourselves.

In the tension between who we are and who we think we want to be, between the world we live in and the world we want to see, God is at work shaping us, transforming us. As we gain greater understanding of who God is and who we are in Him, we see that He will accomplish His purposes through us and despite us. As we learn to trust Him to work through us, we are less anxious to define who we are or to prove our worth. God calls us and sanctifies us to do the work He plans for us to do, and we can rest in His redemption, grace, and renewal.

What if God wants us to see our calling as freedom to live in His grace and trust in His process? This freedom, given to us from His Spirit, means we can just show up—with half-done to-do lists, messy emotions, guilt, and uncertainty—while He grows something beautiful from the soil of who we are, the work of His capable and creative hands.

CALLED FOR MORE

But what about Mother Teresa, Martin Luther King Jr., C. S. Lewis, and the apostle Paul? While I can accept that God can use me as an instrument in small ways, my heart still longs to be used for something greater. It's an elusive desire and hidden hope that I might also do something great for God that has measurable impact. It doesn't help that we are influenced from a young age to believe that we were placed in this world to accomplish some great purpose.

My seven-year-old wants to be a rock star. As soon as she gets home from school, she puts on her favorite dress. The fabric drapes over her shoes and hangs on her too-small frame. But this dress, covered in hot pink and black stars, is what she imagines is the perfect outfit for the famous singer she wants to be. Who am I to tell her that her dream is unrealistic or impossible? If God desired, He could certainly use her as a rock star to glorify Him. But as I see her swallowed up in a too-big dress, I fear that she could get swallowed up in a too-big dream—a dream that is more about finding her own greatness than God's greatness. How do we hold on to our childlike faith that God can accomplish great things through us without getting lost in dreams and losing sight of our identity as His child?

When I was a senior in high school, I felt pressure to know what I wanted to do with the rest of my life. The only image I had of my future was wearing a beret and hopping from coffee shop to coffee shop in a bright and bustling city, where I did work that was meaningful and significant. But I was quickly hit with practical questions from well-meaning adults: "Is it a career that will earn you enough money to pay rent, utilities, and groceries?" Umm . . . what? Suddenly, my future became a lot less bright and a lot more mundane. That deep-down desire to have a special purpose sank like a rock to the bottom of my soul—not entirely lost, but heavy and hidden.

I struggled to reconcile how my calling could be shaped by both practicality and passion. I began to wonder if the concept of finding a God-given calling was just a fantasy fed to me by Disney princesses and well-meaning Sunday School teachers.

Does it seem that everyone around you has figured out the balance of living their practical life while pursuing their passion—and somehow you missed the boat? Whether these are questions you have asked or are asking now, I invite you to consider that a calling is a journey rather than a destination. More, our calling can change to meet different needs in different seasons of life.

Perhaps calling is a cultural construct that is better understood when we look at it as God's calling for us.

> For we are His workmanship, created in Christ Jesus
> for good works, which God prepared beforehand,
> that we should walk in them.
>
> (Ephesians 2:10)

In his Letter to the Ephesians, Paul introduces a concept that turns calling on its head. The world's view of calling places the emphasis on us: our talents, capabilities, vision, and plans for our future. However, Paul's words here remind the Ephesians that God created us as His beautiful and creative creation, summed up in the Greek word *poiema*, meaning "the work made by God." The only other place we see this word is in Romans when Paul says that God's *poiema*, or "the things that have been made [by God]" display "His invisible attributes, namely, His eternal power and divine nature" (Romans 1:20).

Our English word *poem* comes from the Greek word *poiema*. We are God's poem.

In that light, we see that, as His masterpiece, we are designed to fill this place in the world and to accomplish His purpose. While this can sting a bit as our epic role is minimized, it can also be an invitation to relax. Because, as His workmanship, we can trust that every day, whether or not we feel satisfied with who we are and what we are doing, God is going about the work of shaping us into the people He has designed. We can rest in knowing that we can simply abide in Him as He guides us to the roles and places He would have us do His work. Not just "work," but the work that God has already prepared, mapped out, designed specifically for us.

With this knowledge, we can pursue the thing that is causing us to pause and wonder, "What if?" "What if I used this patch of land to plant a community garden for my neighborhood?" "What if I gave in to the urge to put a brush to canvas, even though I've never painted in my life?" "What if I started a book club, signed up to read to children with special needs, learned to bake pies, or volunteered at the community center?" As we see calling as an opportunity to explore rather than pressure to prove our purpose in life, we are freed to let go of our anxieties about our worth and to instead embrace childlike wonder, waiting to see what adventures God is leading us on next.

Too often, we find our purpose in productivity or popularity, but as God's workmanship, we can trust more in the process, the mystery, the things unseen, and the potential. We can trust that God doesn't waste our gifts, passions, or experiences. He

will open and reveal His purposes for us in His just-right timing, like the small rosebud that unfurls into a display of color
and dimension. In a worry-prone world, where we're in a hurry
to have answers, to define and understand or to dismiss, we
can miss the beautiful and undefined things God is doing in
the hidden places of our hearts and in the small and unnoticed
moments where we simply love the people God has placed
before us.

Emily P. Freeman in her book *A Million Little Ways* explores
how God reveals Himself through us in countless small ways.
Rather than waiting and stretching to accomplish the next big
thing, she nudges readers to celebrate the sacred work of
showing up and pouring themselves into the small and unassuming tasks that make up their days. By doing small things
with great love and purpose, we can move through our every
day with more intention, confident that God shines through us.
When we release the pressure to accomplish something big
with our lives, we are freed to see all the little opportunities for
God to be glorified through us. Freeman sums it up well:

> I don't believe there is one great thing I was made to
> do in this world. I believe there is one great God I was
> made to glorify. And there will be many ways, even a
> million little ways, I will declare his glory with my life.[9]

Friend, you are free to grow in God's grace as you embrace
small and everyday ways that your life glorifies God. You are
also free to explore the quiet callings in the corners of your

9   Emily P. Freeman, *A Million Little Ways: Uncover the Art You Were Made to Live* (Grand Rapids, MI: Revell, 2013), 40.

heart—the ones that seem small, insignificant, and unassuming. God tucks His glory in things as small as mustard seeds and wombs. When we worry less about what's big and measurable, we can focus more on God and what He is doing in the small places, trusting Him to grow us, to reveal Himself, and to work all things for our good.

What is growing small inside you? Tremulous, uncertain? A small hope, a secret you're afraid to speak of or look at in the light? Just because you can't see or feel or understand it, doesn't mean it isn't there. How do we grow hope and cradle kingdom dreams in the uniformity of seconds, minutes, and hours . . . laundry, meetings, and deadlines? God isn't restricted by time and tedium. So although we are bogged down by the world's worries and our own need for control, we can cradle hope. The tender shoot that we don't understand, but God can grow and form.

When you believe Paul's assurance that you are God's workmanship, increasing in your understanding that God's own hand shapes and prepares your days and your purpose, I pray that you can begin to release your anxieties over proving your worth to yourself and to the world. I pray that you anticipate the ways God will surprise you and use you.

Maybe my daughter will be a rock star. Maybe she will just glorify God in the car as she sings in wild abandon. As she leans into the small ways that her heart expands, I trust God will lead her to do the things that are big and beautiful too. Whether it's on a stage or in the red dirt of Africa, as she proclaims her faith to an audience or whispers it to comfort her own child,

I can trust that as she abides in Him, she will accomplish His purpose for her life. In this hope for her and for you and for me, I pray that we can rely less on our anxious thoughts and more on God's strength and presence in our lives as a promise that we are His great work.

A MESSY MASTERPIECE

KEY THOUGHT: In our culture, "calling" can feel like a pressure to make something of ourselves, resulting in anxiety and self-doubt. But as we focus our attention on who God is, we feel less anxiety over who we are and more trust that we are becoming who God designed.

Verses for Reflection

For by grace you have been saved through faith. And this is not your own doing; it is the gift of God, not a result of works, so that no one may boast. For we are His workmanship, created in Christ Jesus for good works, which God prepared beforehand, that we should walk in them. (Ephesians 2:8–10)

Glory in His holy name; let the hearts of those who seek the Lord rejoice! Seek the Lord and His strength; seek His presence continually! (Psalm 105:3–4)

Open Your Bible

Read Psalm 139.

Questions to Consider

1. What does David mean in Psalm 105 when he says to "seek the Lord" for strength and for His presence?

   _____

   _____

   _____

   _____

   _____

2. How does this influence the way we live out our calling?

   _____

   _____

   _____

   _____

   _____

3. Ephesians 2 tells us that God has good works that He has prepared for us to walk in. Can you identify ways that God has used you? What did it feel like?

   _____

   _____

   _____

   _____

   _____

4. How do your career and passions influence the way you think about yourself?

_____

_____

_____

_____

_____

5. In Psalm 139, David talks about the intimate way that God knows us. Does this bring you comfort in the face of self-doubt?

_____

_____

_____

_____

_____

6. What are some ways you are able to glorify God in your current circumstances?

_____

_____

_____

_____

_____

Activity

Find a special place to write the word *poiema* where you will see it. This could be on a pot in your garden, a rock that sits on your desk, or on your bathroom mirror. When you feel anxious or uncertain about who you are or what your purpose is, return to this reminder that you are God's great work of art. How will this reminder help you?

_____

_____

_____

_____

_____

CHAPTER 11

EMBRACE GOD'S ADVENTURE

I fell in love with my husband before I met him face-to-face. My spontaneous Michigan boy, with a crooked smile and bright blond hair, had stumbled his way to Concordia Seminary in St. Louis with a hope and a prayer that he could become a Lutheran pastor. At Concordia, he met my brother-in-law, brought together by their mutual love of beer, and immediately hit it off with my sister, because she knew how to cook a hot meal. At their apartment, he glimpsed me among the collection of smiling faces on their family photo wall.

"Who's this? Nathan asked with typical nonchalance.

"That's my little sister," she said between bites.

"Is she single?" he asked with a growing smile and growing interest.

"You two would be a perfect disaster together," she said, wiping her mouth and settling the matter, or so she thought.

My sister's response was exactly what she *shouldn't* have said if she *didn't* want us to wind up together. Accepting the challenge, Nathan found my profile on MySpace. If you've heard of MySpace, then you know it was the cool social platform to connect with friends and friends of friends before Facebook became as popular as peanut butter. When Nathan found my profile and sent me his first charming message, "Hi," neither of us knew that he was actually cracking open the rest of our lives.

Messages over MySpace led to long phone conversations, which led to our first meeting in person, two years later, at the baggage claim in San Diego International Airport. Six months after that, Nathan moved to California, and we took on the hard work of actually being in a relationship. From the start, I knew that he'd have to go back to St. Louis to finish his last year of seminary and that after that, he could be called to a church anywhere in the United States. The knowledge was like a sharp pebble in my shoe, the painful reality surprising me in unexpected moments as I faced the decision before me. But I pushed the thought away, getting swept up in his carefree attitude and love of life. Until, of course, his return to St. Louis was six months away. In a frenzy, we began to make plans. We exchanged vows with big, goofy smiles on our faces and celebrated afterward in a big yellow tent under the setting sun of a warm November evening in San Diego.

It was just enough time for us to get hitched. The very next day, he would drive me and all my stuff to St. Louis. After our beautiful wedding and celebration, I was still in my wedding dress as I sobbed and said good-bye to friends and family whom I wouldn't see again until the following summer. I had always imagined an exotic honeymoon, but ours consisted of stops we made along the route to our new home in Missouri. Nathan loved the adventure, and I was enough in love with him to accept the compromise. Each night, we found the business center at the motel and squeezed onto one chair as we chose the next stop on our journey. Using an online travel agency, we did a blind bid for the next hotel, clicked the button, and closed our eyes as we waited for the picture of the next place we'd be staying to pop up. We did this, making our way from dot to dot on the map, from Las Vegas to Glenwood Springs to Santa Fe to Kansas City.

Instead of worrying about the plans we'd made or ticking off a list of activities we'd scheduled, we were free to be in the moment together. I didn't need to worry if the moments measured up to the expectations I had formed in my head; rather, I took things in with fresh eyes and enjoyed what God provided for us beyond our expectations. In Vegas, we somehow scored a honeymoon suite on our modest budget. Money from wedding gifts allowed us to enjoy romantic meals out, while a timeshare tour scored us tickets to *The Phantom of the Opera* and a five-course meal. We wine-tasted and picnicked and laughed a lot.

My happiest memories are usually enjoying life with the people I love. The formula is pretty simple—life's sweetest moments involve me, plus someone I love, minus my to-do list. If anything, the very best times are when my perfect plan has been foiled. I'm forced to give up my agenda and just let life unfold. It means shedding my perfect plans and vision of what life should be and embracing the adventure of every day.

The Scottish preacher and chaplain Oswald Chambers well

describes this dependence on God:

> To be certain of God means that we are uncertain in
> all our ways; we do not know what a day may bring
> forth. This is generally said with a sigh of sadness; it
> should be rather an expression of breathless expec-
> tation.[10]

Depending on God's plans for our lives can challenge us to shed the expectations that society heaps on us. Have you felt stuck between where you feel God is leading you and what others expect of you? Even when we live a life in tune with the rhythm God calls for us, we can still get stuck in anxious thoughts when we question how we measure up. I invite you to consider that maybe the adventure God wants to take you on means surprising or disappointing people you love. It could mean releasing your own agenda, and it could fly in the face of what the world seems to expect of you. I have a friend who feels God pulling her toward full-time women's ministry, but that would mean leaving her tenured teaching position. I know a man who has the audacious dream of finding a home for every child in the foster care system in our county, and a mom who is returning to college to finish her degree in psychology, at age 37, with the hope of starting a school in Africa.

Maybe God is calling you to something life changing. Or maybe He is calling you to take a smaller step. I know a pediatrician who feels more connected to God when he writes poetry, so he keeps a book of his original Christian poems in the

10   Oswald Chambers, *My Utmost for His Highest* (Grand Rapids, MI: Oswald Chambers Publications Assn., Ltd., 1963), April 29.

reception area of his office.

With God, our answer can be "yes, and." We say "yes" to possibility, "and" we keep our hearts open to the unexpected.

As you turn down the volume of the world's expectations, you will find that you are better able to tune in to God's plan for your life, and it will look as unique as God created you to be. His desires for you may take you by surprise as they prove to be more abundant "than all that [you] ask or think" (Ephesians 3:20), and maybe they will also look different from what others in your life expect.

We can't just push a button and suddenly be transported to a new way of life. This transformative process is a rhythm that develops day by day, even moment by moment, as again and again we return to God and His Word to be reminded of His ways. As you learn the sound of your Shepherd's voice, you will discover that His plans and priorities may contradict the pressures placed on you by media, friends, work, and even family. While we must live in this world and participate in it, a girl seeking God's heart learns that she can't rely on the world's expectations to provide ultimate contentment. But that doesn't mean we don't fall into that trap.

Striving to live the way Chambers describes, a state of "breathless anticipation," we pray for the patience to wait for God's plan to unfold, for faith to overcome fear and anxiety. This doesn't eradicate our anxious thoughts, but it motivates us to redirect them to look for the bigger picture through a God-size lens.

REMEMBER, ABIDE, FIND, *REPEAT*

Paul reminds the Church in Thessalonica what their daily rhythm should look like as they live God's design for their lives:

> Rejoice always, pray without ceasing, give thanks in all circumstances; for this is the will of God in Christ Jesus for you.
>
> (1Thessalonians 5:16–18)

As a writer, I've learned to be careful about the absolute kind of language Paul uses so boldly here. One writing teacher even taught me a phrase to help me remember the importance of such care: "You must always remember in all your work to never write with absolute statements." So, when Paul says, "rejoice always," I cringe a little. And "give thanks in all circumstances"?

It's safe to say that this little verse describes a hard way to live for all humans. I can rejoice, pray, and give thanks sometimes, but my default programming is often grumpy, selfish, and ungrateful. So, what's the deal, Paul? Why is God's will for us so different from our heart's tendency to plan, control, and stress out?

Paul gives us a snapshot of God's desire for our hearts when we live His will for our lives. Through Jesus, we know that we are forgiven and restored in relationship even when we miss the mark, but Paul's words to the Thessalonians provide a useful road map as we look at the life-giving rhythm God desires for our everyday lives.

1. Remember: Rejoice Always

The word *rejoice* means to "feel or show great delight." When I hear the word *rejoice*, I feel I need a choir robe and my hands should be raised in holy hallelujahs. The word has a "churchy" feel to it.

But if we are to "rejoice always," then this is our day in, day out reality—over morning coffee, chores, tax appointments, grocery shopping, and commute to work. But more, "always" means delighting in God in tedium and even in trials, such as a difficult diagnosis, a devastating divorce, relationship conflicts, pandemics, and what we dread most, the death of someone we love.

This doesn't mean we "fake it until we make it," "grin and bear it," or otherwise ignore our sadness and anxieties. "Rejoice always" means even in our grief and anxiety and fear, we remember to praise and thank God for who He is.

When we remember, we see beyond the present moment to reflect on the ways God has been our help in the past and to anticipate the ways He is at work for our future good. "Rejoice always" takes on a melancholy tone as we suffer, but because we know that our Lord turns all things to our good, we can be certain that our suffering is never wasted. The darkness around us makes us clutch our candle close and strain our eyes to see what God is illuminating for us. Sometimes, all we can see is where to take the very next step. "Rejoice always" is an exercise in faith as we remember who God is in good times as well as bad, as we remember that God is bigger than our present circumstances, and as we trust in His plan for us and for all of humanity. It isn't an escape from our reality, but a perspective that shapes how we experience it.

2. Abide: Pray without Ceasing

When I hear "pray without ceasing," I imagine a monk, cloistered and robed, dedicating his life to godliness. I imagine the zealot who stands on the side of the highway with a "Come to Jesus" sign. It is hard to picture what "pray without ceasing" looks like in a society where the social norm is to update social media without ceasing rather than to stay in constant communication with God. When I file this command under "radical," I feel freed to fit in with the mainstream of society that turns to Google for answers to life's most challenging questions (like "what is the best sushi restaurant in my five-mile radius?").

Too often, we keep God at a safe distance throughout the day—shelving prayers for a sacred moment that never seems to come. But what if these words are an invitation and not a command? Here, Paul invites us to depend on God, to stay in touch with Him as our dearest and most loving companion. When I tuck this into my heart as a promise rather than a command, I think of God as a shelter from life's stress and uncertainty and not as an emergency rain poncho stashed in the glove compartment.

We are introduced to the word *abide* in Jesus' teaching to His disciples in John 15:5: "I am the vine; you are the branches. Whoever abides in Me and I in him, he it is that bears much fruit." In our dependence on Jesus, we receive His fullness. *Abide* also means "remain." My most valuable relationships are with the people who have remained beside me when I am at my worst. In the same way, we abide in Jesus through a prayer relationship even when we feel doubtful, disconnected, or disillusioned. In this faithful dependence, we see our hearts change and our lives expand into God's fruitful design. As we hide ourselves in God through prayer and relationship, we turn our anxiousness into reliance. Our anxious thoughts become fervent prayers as we await God's faithful response.

3. Find the Good: Give Thanks

When I feel that my kids are being ungrateful, I can turn this last part of Paul's words for us into a lecture: "God wants us to give thanks in all circumstances! So stop whining and complaining!" I'm sure it's no surprise when I tell you that this isn't the most effective method for overhauling negative attitudes or muting whining and bickering. When I use this same lecture to stop my own ungrateful attitude, it just makes me feel grumpier. When my mind is on an anxious loop, it makes me feel more anxious; I'm plagued with this guilty question: "Why can't I be grateful like I'm supposed to be?"

We can't be forced into a mindset of gratitude. But then how do we "give thanks in all circumstances"? Every afternoon, I walk to school with my four-year-old to pick up my seven-year-old. My four-year-old likes to walk at the pace of Escargot, the snail from our favorite children's book. To motivate her to keep moving, we play a game called "find the good." As we walk, we point out the good things that we see around us. This can be the changing leaves on a tree, a festive wreath on someone's front door, or the way the rain makes the grass sparkle. What started as a simple game has become the pick-me-up I need when I face difficult circumstances.

Now, we find the good on our way to a dreaded doctor's appointment. I help my older daughter find the good after a difficult day at school. I train myself to find the good in a person I'm forming a negative attitude toward. As we identify and name the good in our midst, we are following Paul's advice and God's will to give thanks in all circumstances. It is a habit we train our minds to follow, and as we do, it becomes a new way to see the world. Here's a challenge: Can you have anxious thoughts while you're trying to find the good in a situation? Try it, and experience a moment of relief. Gratitude hushes our harried thoughts as we walk with God and enjoy the world around us.

Of course, in my life, there is no shortage of good things to thank God for, but what about finding good in desperate situations? In Corrie ten Boom's memoir, *The Hiding Place,* Corrie and her sister Betsie are imprisoned at Ravensbrück, a German concentration camp. Faithful to God's call, the Dutch sisters had harbored Jews during World War II, saving many lives but also causing them to be arrested. At Ravensbrück, the Nazis give them flea-infested straw to sleep on. Trying to endure their deplorable living arrangements, Corrie and Betsie pray and give thanks to God for their circumstances. After thanking God for allowing them to remain together, for their smuggled Bible, and for the women there with them, Betsie pushes Corrie to give thanks for the fleas, which Corrie does reluctantly. Months later, the sisters discover that the Nazis don't enter their sleeping quarters because of the fleas! Their flea-infested space gives them more freedom to read their forbidden Bible and to pray with the other women.[11] As we give thanks to God in *all* circumstances, we entrust Him with the situations and the circumstances we don't understand, having faith that He is at work even in the hard things.

Paul's reminder of God's will for our lives guides us to a different way of responding to our world and our thoughts—a way that challenges us to be fully present in our circumstances. Technology and stress and our own flight response cause us to check out of the moment, but Paul invites us to tune in to God and what He is showing us in the circumstance, especially if it clashes with our plans and expectations. As we discipline ourselves to walk with the intention Paul teaches, our thoughts turn to Jesus and His plans for us in the midst of hard circumstances and unexpected detours.

The refrain of the famous hymn "My Hope Is Built on Nothing Less" (LSB 575) by Edward Mote is a strong and hope-filled image:

> On Christ, the solid rock, I stand;
> All other ground is sinking sand.

Jesus is referred to as our rock and cornerstone throughout Scripture, but these verses especially echo a parable of Jesus: "Everyone then who hears these words of Mine and does them will be like a wise man who built his house on the rock" (Matthew 7:24). Our hearts long for security. We seek it in our job, our bank account, our reputation, our children, our

---

11   Corrie Ten Boom, Elizabeth Sherrill, and John Sherrill, *The Hiding Place* (Grand Rapids, MI: Chosen, 2006), 209–211.

spouse, and ourselves, but every one of these things can sink and shift. None of these can bear the weight of our identity or our expectations. Our future lives are uncertain in a world that is constantly changing. But God gives us a promise to stay our unsteady hearts through Jesus and His certain promises of for-giveness and eternal life.

Jesus, fully God, has all power and knowledge. Jesus, Cre-ator of the world and of human life, yet also fully man. In Jesus, we see the complexity and the simplicity of life wrapped into one human package. In Jesus, we see the God who did not see Himself as too great to become one of us, but humbled Himself and broke into His creation to walk in this sin-darkened world.

To this God-man, I release my illusion of control again and again. I am certain of nothing else but Him. So I take a gulp of strong coffee and release a somewhat nervous sigh of hope.

> His oath, His covenant and blood
> Support me in the raging flood;
> When ev'ry earthly prop gives way,
> He then is all my hope and stay.
>
> (LSB 575:3)

EMBRACE GOD'S ADVENTURE

KEY THOUGHT: This life guarantees uncertainty, which can be a recipe for anxiousness. But as plans get messed up, and as our expectations don't measure up, we look to God, who promises security as we rest in His plans and look to our secure future with Him.

Verses for Reflection

Rejoice always, pray without ceasing, give thanks in all circumstances; for this is the will of God in Christ Jesus for you. (1 Thessalonians 5:16–18)

Abide in Me, and I in you. As the branch cannot bear fruit by itself, unless it abides in the vine, neither can you, unless you abide in Me. I am the vine; you are the branches. Whoever abides in Me and I in him, he it is that bears much fruit, for apart from Me you can do nothing. (John 15:4–5)

Open Your Bible

Read Ephesians 3:14–21.

Questions to Consider

1. Which part of 1 Thessalonians 5:16–18 do you find the most challenging to live out? How are you going to try to approach it differently?

    _____

    _____

    _____

    _____

    _____

2. How has life not been going as planned? How are you coping?

    _____

    _____

    _____

    _____

    _____

3. Ephesians 3 talks about God's power at work within us. How does this transform your perspective about your own plans in light of what God is capable of?

    _____

    _____

    _____

    _____

    _____

4. What is the role of the vine in relationship to the branches? How does this image teach us about what it looks like to abide?

_____

_____

_____

_____

_____

5. How are you abiding in Jesus?

_____

_____

_____

_____

_____

Activity

Write Ephesians 3:20–21 below and commit it to memory. Take a quiet moment to pray it by yourself or with a group as you trust in "Him who is able" (v. 20).

_____

_____

_____

_____

_____

_____

_____

CHAPTER 12

COMFORTED TO COMFORT

I asked my social media community to fill in the blank for this statement:

> *When I experience anxious thoughts, it makes me feel*
>
> _____.

Within five minutes, I'd received an overwhelming response. Overwhelmed, isolated, afraid, inadequate, and misunderstood were among the answers that flooded in—all echoing the same helpless frustration.

What do you feel when you experience anxious thoughts?

I nod my head to every answer above. Anxious thoughts make me feel every one of those feelings and more. But when I began sharing my experience with anxiety, and the way it has affected my identity and faith, I started feeling the Holy Spirit redirecting my perspective to look at things through a bigger lens. My hope as you conclude this book is that you will see how God is about the work of redeeming the difficult parts of your story as you grow in faith and perspective, even as you continue to battle anxious thoughts.

Paul compares us to clay pots, ordinary yet fragile, designed to contain something greater than ourselves. It's humbling to think of myself as a clay pot, but then I read on to see that because of what I contain, I cannot be broken.

> But we have this treasure in jars of clay, to show that the surpassing power belongs to God and not to us. We are afflicted in every way, but not crushed; perplexed, but not driven to despair; persecuted, but not forsaken; struck down, but not destroyed.

(2 Corinthians 4:7–9)

The Greek word Paul uses for "afflicted" is *thlipsis,* which also means "pressure that causes someone to feel confined or restricted." Anxious thoughts make us feel hopeless, helpless, and out of control. But in light of this verse, we are reminded that afflictions of this world cannot crush our fragile frame, because God's glory is at work within us.

But how do we access this strength as we feel overwhelmed, isolated, afraid, inadequate, and misunderstood under the pressure of our anxious thoughts? As we have explored throughout this book, we know that God's Spirit dwells within us. In the midst of our desperate emotions, we have continual access to God through prayer and through His Word. This strength comes from faith in Jesus, a gift of God by the power of the Spirit, received through the Word and assured in Baptism. This strength is renewed as we spend time in His Word and is strengthened in a special way when we come to the Lord's Table to receive the assurance that His love and forgiveness are for us.

> Blessed be the God and Father of our Lord Jesus
> Christ, the Father of mercies and God of all comfort,
> who comforts us in all our affliction.
>
> (2 Corinthians 1:3–4)

The word *comfort* throughout the New Testament means something greater than just receiving sympathy. Paul uses the Latin root *fortis,* meaning strength and power, to give us a a deeper understanding of God's comfort. Another word that stems from the Latin root *fortis* is *fort*. God provides us not only with inner strength but also with a place we can run to as our refuge.

> Be to me a rock of refuge, to which I may continually
> come.
>
> (Psalm 71:3)

While all can experience God's love, His comfort is something that is uniquely experienced in suffering. This means that as we turn to God with our *thlipsis,* or afflictions, we get to experience His strength in place of our weakness. To go deeper, we consider that as jars of clay, when the affliction grows greater in force, pressing in all around us, the glory of God is magnified as it pushes out in our protection.

Stronger Still

Squeeze, beat, crash, and shake,
Whatever the pressure, it cannot break
Our fragile vessels made of clay,
Because of the strength that we contain.

Though fear thuds loud,

Though worry wears,

Though others try to strike me down,

God's presence, strength, and comfort be

All the greater within me.

(by Lindsay Hausch)

GOD'S UPSIDE-DOWN BLESSING

I have heard Christians approach anxious thoughts with the refrain "have more faith," as if a person can squeeze shut her eyes and expand her faith by sheer will. However, I believe that in order to know the "faith that moves mountains," we must also know the doubt that could undo us. We see in 2 Corinthians that suffering, struggle, and anxiety can actually lead us to the comfort and power of God when we turn to Him. Jesus, in the Sermon on the Mount, introduces an upside-down kingdom that shows us that God honors us in our struggles and humility:

Blessed are the poor in spirit,
for theirs is the kingdom of heaven.

Blessed are those who mourn,
for they shall be comforted.

Blessed are the meek,
for they shall inherit the earth.
(Matthew 5:3–5)

In Jesus' upside-down kingdom, the things we might try to overcome, forget, or altogether avoid, are the very places where we experience blessedness:

200

Blessed are the pure in heart, for they shall see God.

(Matthew 5:8)

In this upside-down culture, it is in the uncertainty, doubt, and struggle that we have the opportunity to seek and experience God's grace. With this understanding, we can see doubt and anxious thoughts as the pit into which we fall or as the bridge that takes us to God, His comfort, His strength, and greater faith.

Consider the moments when you turn to God most. Is it when your job is secure, your kids are well behaved, your marriage is peaceful, and the bank account is full? If I'm honest, when life feels secure, I often rely on that state for my peace of mind. I want to be the girl who is constantly in a rhythm of reliance on God, but in reality, I turn to Him and pray more when life is complicated and the future is uncertain.

None of us will escape this life without experiencing doubt, worry, uncertainty, struggle, and loss. While I can write about all the ways we can overcome our anxious thoughts, the truth is that there are times when we will have no choice but to walk through them.

When our anxieties become our realities, the way ahead seems uncertain.

But Jesus knows this well. That is why He reminds us that life will involve suffering:

In the world you will have tribulation.

But His warning comes with the Good News that transforms

our experience:

> But take heart; I have overcome the world.
>
> (John 16:33)

Since we have a new vocabulary word, I can point out that Jesus uses a form of the word *thlipsis* to describe the struggle that lies ahead for His followers. Yet rather than saying that He has overcome our *thlipsis,* He says He has "overcome the world." Why is this? Our tribulation, suffering, afflictions, worries, fears—all these are symptoms, not the source of what ails us. Jesus overcomes the fallen world so that He can have a relationship with us and be our comfort now and one day set the world right again.

Hours after Jesus warns His disciples that they will face tribulation, they witness the greatest tragedy imaginable. The Messiah, in whom they had put their trust and risked everything to follow, doesn't overcome and conquer the world as they had expected. Instead, He is mocked, beaten, and brutally killed on a cross. His body is broken. And the disciples think all His promises are also broken. It seems that Jesus has been overcome by the cruel world rather than the other way around.

"But take heart," dear friends. The God who came to earth to redeem us and restore our relationship with Him leaves no stone unturned. Three days later, the women come with spices to anoint Jesus' body, but "they [find] the stone rolled away from the tomb" (Luke 24:2). Two angels stand by and ask them, "Why do you seek the living among the dead? He is not here, but has risen" (Luke 24:5–6).

Jesus, God in flesh, has overcome the world by overcoming death itself. Yes, against the desolate landscape of pain and hopelessness, God shows His power and life. In the process, the disciples' view of Jesus expands from seeing Him as the Messiah who would deliver them from the Romans to the Messiah who would deliver them from sin, from death, and from the evil one. Jesus faced the world's greatest affliction in order to reveal God's greatest glory.

As the Bible takes us face to face with grief, suffering, and death, it also delivers to us a hope that has no better package: God became man to overcome death and to bring us life in a decaying world. In the light of this reality, we don't dismiss anxiousness or even suffering, because we believe that God, who overcame death itself, will overcome everything that causes us worry. This means that our places of anxiety and suffering are the very places we may see God's hand at work. Rather than an ideology that tells us to escape, minimize, cure, or ignore our struggle, we can turn to God Himself, who comes to us in our place of struggle and uncertainty and offers Himself.

WHEN WE FACE OUR FEARS

There are the everyday sort of anxious thoughts, and then there are the ones that come with deep suffering and uncertainty. The worry that keeps you up at night as you wait for the test results that could be the wrecking ball to your current reality. The ruminations that descend as you contemplate whether you can stay committed to your marriage vows. The anxious swirl of grief and heartache as you lose someone you love. These are the moments when the anxious "what if?" transforms into "what now?" as we navigate struggles that take us into unfamiliar territory.

In face of the unexpected, as we wait on God, we are challenged to go from discussing our theology to living it out. Doubt, disappointment, or disaster can cause us to ask: *Do I really trust God? Am I living like it?*

It is easy to become consumed with the everyday noise of our lives. We can be so consumed with everyday living that we don't consider the big life questions that determine who we are and how we live. But in the face of life's difficult realities, the busy hum gets quieted as real life crashes upon us and forces us to reckon with it. It is often in this collision with reality that we are forced to move from what we believe in theory to how we live what we believe. In life's struggles, theology is no longer the subject of debate or the creed we say sleepily on Sunday morning. Rather, it is the truth we desperately grab hold of as we slip over the edge of our once-normal life. The Holy Spirit is no longer the topic we explore in sermons and Sunday school lessons but God's comfort and courage in seemingly impossible circumstances.

For many Christians, transformation takes place in the midst of struggle, when their faith becomes more than a belief system—it becomes their lifeline.

But does it really first take a catastrophe in order to experience this kind of faith formation? Since you have picked up this book, you may be living with a tension that stirs you to want more of God. Like my social media friends who commented on my post, you are able to fill in the blank with your own difficult experience of how anxious thoughts make you feel. Your original question when you picked up this book might have been "How can God help me to overcome my anxious thoughts?" But by now, I hope you have had a shift in perspective to see that anxious thoughts can be the very struggle that drives you to God.

But there is more to the story. In our anxiety and struggle, we experience God's supernatural comfort, which equips us to comfort others. Earlier, we explored 2 Corinthians 1:3, and the first half of verse 4. The second half of the verse is just as essential and transformational. For clarity, let's look at the entire text:

> Blessed be the God and Father of our Lord Jesus
> Christ, the Father of mercies and God of all comfort,
> who comforts us in all our affliction, so that we may
> be able to comfort those who are in any affliction,
> with the comfort which we ourselves are comforted
> by God.
>
> (2 Corinthians 1:3–4)

As I said in the first chapter, I believe that when we turn to God with our anxious thoughts, He is not only with us as we suffer, providing peace and strength, but He also calls and equips us to be His ambassadors of hope to anxious people. Since every human experiences anxious thoughts, our own struggle is a training ground for loving and helping a world of worriers.

What does this look like in your community? It will be different for each of us. But it is essential to start with honesty. That is, we don't just share our victories; we are honest about the struggle, doubt, fear, isolation, and setbacks. Christians celebrate the empty tomb because we know the depth of Christ's suffering. His victory is all the greater because of Good Friday. As we are honest about our own struggle with anxious thoughts and the comfort we receive in Jesus, the comfort we offer others becomes vulnerable and real.

The depth of strength and comfort we receive in relationship with God is a treasure we cannot contain within ourselves. In life's uncertainty, in the midst of an anxious world, we are overwhelmed by our Comforter, the Holy Spirit. Since the core of God's identity from the beginning of time is relationship as Father, Son, and Holy Spirit, God's Spirit beckons us to share the comfort and fullness we receive in relationship with others as we bring God's promises to an anxious and hurting world.

COMFORTED TO COMFORT

KEY THOUGHT: Our doubt and struggle are the very places where God's Spirit builds our faith as He comforts us and equips us to comfort a hurting world.

Verses for Reflection

But we have this treasure in jars of clay, to show that the surpassing power belongs to God and not to us. We are afflicted in every way, but not crushed; perplexed, but not driven to despair; persecuted, but not forsaken; struck down, but not destroyed. (2 Corinthians 4:7–9)

Blessed be the God and Father of our Lord Jesus Christ, the Father of mercies and God of all comfort, who comforts us in all our affliction, so that we may be able to comfort those who are in any affliction, with the comfort with which we ourselves are comforted by God. (2 Corinthians 1:3–4)

Open Your Bible

Read Matthew 5:2–12.

Questions to Consider

1. Second Corinthians 4:8–9 says we are afflicted, perplexed, and persecuted as believers. What do these words mean? How have you experienced them?

   _____

   _____

   _____

   _____

   _____

2. How has God protected you from being crushed, desperate, and destroyed? How would you share this experience with others?

   _____

   _____

   _____

   _____

   _____

3. In Matthew 5, Jesus shares what's known as the Beatitudes in the Sermon on the Mount. How have you experienced God's upside-down kingdom in your own life? How does this help you to think differently about difficult experiences?

   _____

   _____

   _____

   _____

   _____

4. Have you received God's comfort in a time of anxiousness or struggle? If so, how can you offer the comfort you have received to your community?

_____

_____

_____

_____

_____

5. Has this book helped you think about anxious thoughts in a new way?

_____

_____

_____

_____

Activity

On a small clay pot, write a Bible verse that comforts you. When you experience an anxious thought, write it on a small strip of paper and put it into the pot. As you place each one, pray over the situation, and pray that God would comfort you to be a comfort to others.

_____

_____

_____

_____

_____

ANSWERS

CHAPTER 1

1. As Christians, we believe that God the Father offered His Son, Jesus, as an atoning sacrifice for the sin that comes between us and God. Through Jesus' sacrificial death on our behalf, and because He brings us into relationship with God through the sacrament of Holy Baptism, we have faith in Jesus as our Lord and Savior.

2. Answers will vary. Naming your "anxiety inducers" can be helpful, either aloud to a group or on your own in a journal. They don't have to seem "valid," because anxious thoughts like to burrow in our mind over seemingly mundane things. If you need inspiration, here's a list of things that induce Lindsay's anxiety: travel, a messy house, hosting new people at her house, running late, ruminating over how others think or feel about her, crowds, noisy places, when Nathan doesn't wash his late-night snack dishes (kidding . . . mostly).

3. Answers will vary.

4. David tells Saul he used to strike down lions and bears that would steal sheep from his father's flock.

5. Answers will vary.

6. Answers will vary. The question invites readers to consider that God can use our gifts and past experiences to equip us to do greater and unexpected things. One example is that Lindsay was an ad writer for beauty products, which led her to becoming a Christian writer.

CHAPTER 2

1. "In repentance and rest is your salvation, in quietness and trust is your strength" (Isaiah 30:15 NIV). The New International Version provides insight in its translation of the word "returning" as "repentance." Repentance means turning back to God with confession of the ways we have fallen short and with a desire to turn from our negative and destructive behaviors. In repentance, we receive through Jesus forgiveness, salvation, and rest that comes from relationship with God.

2. Answers will vary.

3. The "one thing" is Jesus. Mary chooses to focus on sitting at His feet and learning from Him.

4. Jesus invites Martha to consider what she gives her thoughts and attention to most, and we are invited to do the same.

5. Rest is an act of worship and obedience, but it can also come from doing the things that give us energy and joy.

6. Answers will vary but may include resting, reading God's Word, and prayer.

CHAPTER 3

1. We are made in the image of God, that is, eternal. Because of this, man longs for the eternal. Knowing that God is constant and never changes can center our hearts and minds as we abide in Him through rest and can help us find respite from a world that is constantly changing and pulling us to try to keep up.

2. A yoke is a wooden bar that fits over the necks of two animals (primarily oxen) and attaches to the cart for them to pull. This image does not automatically conjure an image of rest, but it illustrates a life lived with God as our master and our navigator. He does not leave us to pull the heavy load by ourselves. Rather, we are to rest as we trust Him to lead and guide our steps.

3. When we recognize that God is God and we are not, we recognize that we are powerless to effect change without His strength, guidance, and also His rest.

4. Answers will vary.

5. Answers will vary.

6. Answers will vary.

CHAPTER 4

1. Answers will vary.

2. The world promises peace that is based on humans and human emotions. It can offer us only temporary comfort. The peace Jesus brings, however, is an eternal solution to sin and death. God is unchanging and trustworthy, while the world is unpredictable and fickle. More, because of Jesus, we can receive the Holy Spirit, who brings us His supernatural peace and guidance.

3. Other translations call the Holy Spirit different names, including Comforter, Helper, Advocate, Counselor, Companion, and Friend.

4. Paul helps us see that Holy Spirit we receive through Jesus is the same Spirit that restored Jesus to life according to God's plan for salvation. We can therefore trust that this Spirit will give us eternal life also.

5. Answers will vary.

6. Answers will vary.

CHAPTER 5

1. Jesus is the founder of our faith, because it is through His life, death, and resurrection that we have relationship with God our Father. Through faith in Jesus, the Holy Spirit dwells in us and helps us to grow more and more into God's image.

2. Answers will vary.

3. Sanctification is important because it speaks to our journey in faith with Jesus, which is never stagnant, but through the Holy Spirit, is ever growing and changing to make us more like Jesus.

4. Answers will vary.

5. Answers may vary, but we see it is through Peter's relationship with Jesus and through the wisdom and confidence provided by the Holy Spirit.

6. Answers will vary.

CHAPTER 6

1. Answers will vary.

2. Answers will vary.

3. The verses instruct us to make our prayers about intimacy and relationship with God rather than something performative for others to see.

4. In David's song of thanks, David guides readers to give thanks to God, to call upon His name, and to share Him with others. David also encourages us to sing praises to God and to seek Him and His strength and presence continually. Worship, thanksgiving, and seeking the Lord are important aspects of a life of relationship and prayer with God.

5. Paul instructs us to remember that our battle is not physical but spiritual. Our ultimate defense and weapon in spiritual warfare is confident prayer in Jesus' name.

6. Answers will vary.

CHAPTER 7

1. We receive grace and forgiveness through Jesus and then are able to extend that to others in relationship. This means pushing past our own sinful feelings to try to view others through the lens of God's compassion and love.

2. Jesus, God incarnate, entered into relationship with hurting and marginalized people. He showed compassion and help while inviting them to live life in Him. This can challenge and encourage us to engage with "the least of these" (Matthew 25:40).

3. When Jesus is told His mother and brothers are waiting outside, He responds, "Here are My mother and My brothers! For whoever does the will of God, he is My brother and sister and mother" (Mark 3:30–31). Answers will vary, but Mark 3 shows us a different picture of how to define family.

4. Answers will vary.

5. Answers will vary.

6. Answers will vary.

CHAPTER 8

1. Answers will vary.

2. Answers will vary.

3. First John challenges us to love not just in what we say but also in the way we live.

4. Answers will vary.

5. Answers will vary.

6. Answers will vary.

CHAPTER 9

1. Synonyms for *restoration* include *repair* and *rehabilitation*. Paul challenges the Corinthians (and us) to strive to make their relationships right through reconciliation to the best of their ability. This can mean apologizing, listening, and forgiving when our heightened emotions compel us to remain in conflict.

2. When we are in the position to offer counsel or mediation, it can be tempting to engage in gossip or offer self-serving advice. Paul reminds the Gentiles, and us, to be careful.

3. Answers will vary.

4. Answers will vary.

5. Answers will vary.

CHAPTER 10

1. We seek God in His Word, in prayer, and in worship. David's Psalm reminds us that we can do this as part of our daily rhythm. Often, we make our relationship with God about what we do, but David reminds us the importance of abiding.

2. Answers will vary.

3. Answers will vary.

4. In Psalm 139, David writes that God "knows our thoughts from afar" and that He is "acquainted with all your (our) ways" (v. 2–3). More, David revels that God "formed my (our) inward parts." We can be comforted by David's confidence in how well God knows each of us.

5. Answers will vary.

CHAPTER 11

1. Answers will vary.

2. Answers will vary.

3. In Ephesians 3:14–21, Paul prays for spiritual strength for the Ephesians and reminds them of God's power at work within them and us.

4. The vine is the life source of the branches; we cannot grow unless we are connected to Jesus. Abiding means acknowledging our need for Jesus as our source of strength and life.

5. Answers will vary but can include reading God's Word, praying, and finding time for rest.

CHAPTER 12

1. Synonyms for *afflicted* include *troubled, oppressed, distressed*. Synonyms for *perplexed* include *bewildered, confused, baffled*. Synonyms for *persecuted* include *mistreated, victimized, punished*.

2. Answers will vary.

3. Answers will vary.

4. Answers will vary.

5. Answers will vary.

REFERENCES

DeVries, John. *Why Pray?* Grand Rapids, MI: Mission India, 2005

Gottman, John M. *The Relationship Cure*. New York: Three Rivers Press, 2002.

Hunter, John. *Knowing God's Secrets*. Fort Washington, PA: CLC Publications, 2011.

Library of Congress. "The American Colony in Jerusalem— Family Tragedy." Exhibitions. Accessed September 8, 2019. https://loc.gov/exhibits/americancolony/amcolony-family.html/.

Walters, Natalie. "The fascinating story of how 2 brothers went from running a failing business out of a van to building a $100 million company," *Business Insider*, February 3, 2016. https://www.businessinsider.com/the-success-story-of-life-is-good-2016-2/.

Williams, Matthew. "Shame Removed; Honor Received." *The Good Book Blog, Biola University*, June 17, 2011. https://www.biola.edu/blogs/good-book-blog/2011/shame-removed-honor-received-part-3/.